T0365208

THE
HANDBOOK
—— FOR ——
LEARNING
—— AND ——
DEVELOPMENT
PROFESSIONALS

Dr. K. Dave Crowder

THE HANDBOOK FOR LEARNING AND DEVELOPMENT PROFESSIONALS

iUniverse books may be ordered through booksellers or by contacting:

iUniverse
1663 Liberty Drive
Bloomington, IN 47403
www.iuniverse.com
1-800-Authors (1-800-288-4677)

ISBN: 978-1-5320-8691-5 (sc)
ISBN: 978-1-5320-8690-8 (e)

Library of Congress Control Number: 2019920829

Print information available on the last page.

iUniverse rev. date: 01/09/2020

TABLE OF CONTENTS

DEDICATION

TO MY PARENTS, Ken and Joan, without whom I would have never accomplished what I have in life and certainly would not have been able to write this book. My mother and father instilled the values of learning, dedication, commitment, and hard work into both me and my sister throughout our lives. It was these values that led me to gain the education and work experience I have. Without those attributes, this book could never have been written. I will be forever grateful to them.

And to the memory of a dear friend, April Story. April was an intelligent, attractive, and athletic woman with a wonderful sense of humor. She had a great spirit and was able to light up any room and bring smiles to everyone's faces. She was an amazing person who was taken from this world far too soon. The world is a lesser place without her.

April Story: April 19, 1962–September 24, 2008

FOREWORD

WHILE COMPLETING THE required courses to achieve my professional accounting designation, my focus was entirely on passing (with a decent grade, if possible). I knew that I did better in some subjects than others because of my own level of interest and/or ability. But I was also keenly aware that in the traditional formal format of a lecture, the quality of instruction was painfully diverse.

I really had no concept of the plethora of instructional methodologies and theory behind the learning and development discipline that are delineated in *The Handbook for Learning and Development Professionals*. I believe most of my above-mentioned lecturers had no idea either. The good ones undoubtedly knew how to present the course material in a way that resonated with the class, resulting in better content retention, but many were not trained educators; their teaching styles were borne of their own work and life experiences. Was the difference between the good ones and the bad ones innate talent, a studied methodology, trial and error, or some combination thereof? I opt for the latter.

Throughout my career in financial services, primarily in reinsurance, I have attended countless seminars, courses, retreats, conferences, summits, and symposiums, both internal and external. These have covered technical topics on underwriting, capital utilization methodologies, International Financial Reporting Standards (IFRS), IT systems training, and government regulations (incessantly), to name but a few. The vast majority of the training I encountered was on soft topics—leadership, interviewing, management (staff, clients, time, resources), conflict resolution, goal setting, achievement, and much more. My evaluation of their value to and effectiveness for me and for the organization would vary from two to nine on a scale of ten, with the majority achieving a five or above. Company resources must be deployed in training and development more efficiently and effectively than that.

Personally, I have found that the most effective management and educational approach is situational, where possible. It is best to work with the individual strengths and aptitudes of your people to achieve common corporate goals.

I have known David Crowder for more than forty years. He is a consummate professional and a tireless pursuer of practical education on behalf of his employers. This handbook that David has written is a veritable trove of useful insights into, and commentary on, the vast educational resources at the disposal of the learning and development professional. This compendium may be used as a reference when undertaking new initiatives to source the most effective and efficient means of delivering the needed education.

Kenneth B. Irvin, CPA, CGA
President and Chief Executive Officer (Ret.), Munich Reinsurance Company of Canada

PREFACE

WHEN I FIRST entered the learning and development (L & D) field, I was like most everyone else I've met in this field. People who work in learning and development typically come from the industry they are working in, and their expertise is in the type of business the company is in. I was a plant operator in a chemical plant, and I was known for doing a good job of training new operators, so I was promoted to the role of plant training coordinator. From my experience I would say the typical learning and development professional is a hardworking person who is promoted into the role from another role within his or her respective business.

The problem is that the field of education is not this person's area of expertise, as it was not mine when I entered into the training coordinator role. The problem becomes that the new learning and development role is half technical and half educational. If our companies hired people whose expertise was in the education field, well, that wouldn't work as those people would know very little about the business—and knowing the business end is vital.

Most learning and development people I have had the pleasure of meeting in this field have become exceptionally knowledgeable in the specific area(s) of the educational field they are working in, but it was in most cases a long, hard journey. When I first entered the field, I was given a three-day train-the-trainer course, but that was it. I remember looking for a good book that would cover all the basics, but no such volume existed. In order to learn about each area of the education field, I started taking university courses in the evening. One thing led to another, and I completed a bachelor of education degree. Luckily, I had tremendous support from my managers: Wes Yeo, Prasad Puttagunta, Cecil Miller, and Denis Bisson. After moving on to another company, I completed my master's and doctor of education degrees, again thanks to tremendous support from my managers—thanks, Michael Crothers, Brian Pritchard, and Chris Schultz. Upon completing my doctor of education, I still thought a book covering all the basics of the educational field would be valuable for managers of learning and development groups, for everyone working within a learning and development group, and especially for anyone newly entering the learning and development field. Hence, I wrote *The Handbook for Learning and Development Professionals*; I hope you all find it an interesting and valuable resource.

Throughout the book, I have tried to include some of my experiences from more than twenty-five years of working in and managing learning and development in both industry and corporate settings. While the book does cover all the basics, it is written from a corporate and industry learning perspective. That's not to say an educator in the teaching field would not find the book of value. I think such a person will find the book to be a very good reference.

As I just stated, this book would have never come to fruition if I had not received the formal education I had, and that would not have happened without the support of the managers I previously thanked. I'm also thankful to have worked for Agrium (formerly Sherritt Gordon), Dow Chemical, Shell, and Devon Energy, all of which are international companies with a strong focus on employee development. They all gave me a great environment in which to learn and apply my learning.

Education, and learning and development (L & D) is such an amazing field. In writing this book I have had so many professionals in the learning field share with me their stories and expertise. Our field is different from most other fields of study. A person who is not an engineer but who works at an engineering firm in some capacity cannot go take a second- or third-year university engineering course and expect to be successful. Engineering, the sciences, and most similar fields of study are like tall buildings; you cannot build the third floor of a tall building unless the first and second floors are already in place. Likewise, you cannot build the forty-sixth floor unless the first forty-five floors are already built, and so on. But education, learning, and development are not at all like a tall building. The education field is more like a building with the same square footage of floor space as the tall building, but with over three-fourths of it only one story tall, a few sections two stories, and maybe some small sections three stories high—and that is it. Mind you, like the tall building of study, it still needs a solid foundation and footings upon which to be built. For the most part a person can build on any one area of the educational learning field and become an expert in that area while having little to no expertise in the other segments of the field (building).

In writing this book I've met people with no university degree, or with a degree but not in the education field, who were very knowledgeable in some aspects of the L & D field. They studied it, in most cases via self-study, and they gained a great deal of experience through their work. That's the beauty of our field; all the knowledge equates to a huge building, but there's no twelfth floor requiring eleven floors of knowledge first. You can begin building from the foundation you have in any area, build a beautiful section of knowledge, and live there. You can then develop by building more extensions in any direction onto the base of your current knowledge. This demonstrates how vast and diverse the education field is. My hope is that *The Handbook for Learning and Development Professionals* will provide what any practitioner needs to build upon in any area of the education field.

I have written the book so each chapter can be read separately. You do not have to read chapter 1 to understand chapter 2, or the first four chapters to understand chapter 5, and so on. I have used a learning objects approach where each chapter can stand on its own but also relates to all the other chapters. Read what chapters interest you, and use each chapter as a reference in your work. Each chapter is meant to provide the basics of a topic in the educational field. Each chapter will provide a practitioner with enough knowledge to discuss the topic intelligently with anyone. Bear in mind, however, that each chapter is just a small elucidation of what could be one or more two-hundred-plus-page textbooks on the topic. This book aims to supply the basics and some real-life examples to enable the reader to gain a good understanding of each topic.

I have read too many education-based books to count—I'm not boasting; I am just stating an occupational hazard. In many of the chapters I have recommended books I feel are like the educational bibles on the topic. If you find your work taking you deep into one these areas, I highly recommend you further your development through purchasing and studying the text suggested. Besides, nothing is quite as impressive as a good private library collection.

Finally, I have written a few chapters that are part of the learning and development professional's field but are not explicitly focused on a specific area in the educational field. Did I mention the field is broad and diverse? There are chapters on leadership and project management, and these are certainly areas that corporate and industry learning and development professionals will be involved with. Neither my theory on learning mastery or the chapter on myths in the educational field is written on a specific area of the educational field, but I believe they are of value to any educator or learning and development professional in performing his or her function.

CHAPTER 1

The Myths

INTRODUCTION

THE REAL POINT of this chapter is not to identify all the myths out there related to learning and then to debunk them. I simply want to point out that there is a lot of codswallop out there, and as an educator or learning and development professional, you need to be wary of what's been marketed and carefully evaluate learning approaches and their claims.

LEARNING STYLES

I CAN THINK of no other topic in education and learning and development that gets so much attention. There is no universally agreed-upon definition as to precisely what a learning style is. There are at least seventy-one different models for learning styles (Scott 2010). The most widely known and used among these include Kolb's (1984) model with four learning styles (converger, diverger, assimilator, accommodator); Honey and Mumford's (1982) four-way typology learning styles model (activist, reflector, theorist, pragmatist); Grasha and Riechmann's (1974) cognitive approach with six learning styles (avoidant, participative, competitive, collaborative, dependent, independent); and probably the most widely known and used, VARK learning styles by Fleming and Mills (1987), which emphasizes visual, auditory, read/write, and kinesthetic learning styles. A learner's preferred learning style is determined by having the student complete a learning styles inventory (questionnaire). Once a learner's learning style is identified, instruction is geared toward that style or delivered covering all styles so everyone in a class is covered. The theory is that learners will learn best when taught in their preferred learning style.

I think there is a lot of energy and belief in learning styles because a lot of people would like to think we're all (especially children) intelligent people with an equal ability to learn, and if someone is a slow learner it is because the wrong learning style is being used, not because the person is less intelligent. A wonderfully idealistic thought, but sadly people do have different intelligence levels and different aptitudes for different areas of study. Learning styles have been studied since the early 1970s, and not one study has supported the idea that a person learns better with any particular learning style. For every given topic there are slower learners, and there is nothing learning styles can do about it. All is not lost, however, as I will explain in chapter 5. But don't get your hopes up too high; there is no magic bullet like learning styles are purported to be.

I know right now you may be disagreeing; you are convinced

you have a certain learning style, or you have seen student success after applying learning styles in your teaching. Or when you were earning your bachelor of education degree, a professor taught you all about learning styles, and you wrote a paper praising them and received an A+. Sadly, there are a lot of professors (supposed experts) who still believe in and teach this myth. As Scott (2010) stated in her research study, university education departments continue to teach learning styles to future teachers, seemingly unaware of the overwhelming amount of evidence against their having any value in instructional design. For those still convinced of learning styles efficacy, let me try to convince you with what real peer-reviewed research evidence shows.

The research that supports learning styles (and there is a great deal of it) all follows the same experimental design. Students are given a pretest, then the researchers determine each person's learning style with a questionnaire, and then each person is taught in their preferred learning style. Then a posttest is completed, and the results show all the participants learned a significant amount. Therefore, learning styles work. However, when research is done where some learners are taught in their learning style and others are taught not using their learning style, researchers find all the students still learn just as much. There is no difference. Examples of this type of study and findings, to list a few, have been completed by DeTure (2004), Fahy and Ally (2005), Kanuka and Nocente (2003), Moan and Dereshiwsky (2002), Price (2004), Santo (2001), Schellens and Valcke (2000), and Terrell (2002, 2003). A study by Duff and Duffy (2002) examined Kolb's (1984) and Honey and Mumford's (1982) learning styles and found no evidence that the two bipolar dimensions proposed by Kolb exist. They found no relationship between the learning style scales and academic performance. Furthermore, Garner (2000) looked at learning style inventories (questionnaires) and found that retesting for Kolb's learning styles did not reliably produce the same results. I could go on and on, but I will finish with the concluding statement from Scott's (2010, 14) research on learning styles, namely that "the continuing endorsement of 'learning styles' wastes teaching and learning time, promotes damaging stereotypes about individuals, and interferes with the development of evidence-based best practice. It has no place in education theory and practice."

Despite the overwhelming evidence to the contrary, you are likely still not convinced because you have seen student success since you have implemented the learning styles approach in your classroom. Well, here is why, and this is good news if you now realize learning styles are bunk and you are feeling down because you're thinking you need to redesign all your current teaching approaches that are based on learning styles. We know repetition is good for learning; we also know repetition leads to boredom— and boredom is bad for learning. So teaching a topic with several different exercises, one designed for cognitive learners, one designed for kinesthetic learners, one designed for visual learners, one designed for audio learners, and so on, creates repetition, which is good for learning, and by mixing the approaches up, you have a built-in strategy for combating boredom. That is why there is success in using a learning styles approach, but the success comes from repetition with low boredom and is not the result of different approaches reaching different learners with different learning styles! The key is knowing the reason for success, and that is that the different approaches create variety.

If you are focused on different approaches based on learning styles, you might, for example, experience what I have as a student. You come back to a course after lunch, and the instructor goes into a lecture (and you are fighting not to fall asleep with your heavy lunch digesting away). Later in the afternoon when your lunch has digested and you are not feeling so lethargic, the instructor does a kinesthetic-type exercise that gets you up, standing and/or moving about. The instructor is going through different approaches to cover all the learning styles. A teacher who knows she is using different approaches for variety would know to do the kinesthetic-type exercise after lunch and to do the lecture early in the day. Forget learning styles, but take the lesson they provide and create variety in your teaching. Use learning styles as a way to create variety and limit boredom, not as a way to limit and pigeonhole learners.

ROLE PLAY

THE IDEA BEHIND role play is fairly straightforward. Students learn something in the classroom, and then they practice it in a role-play situation. For example, students may learn about how to handle conflict. The students are given a scenario and are assigned roles to play. In this example one student will be assigned the role of being the source of the conflict, and another student will play the role of the person who resolves the conflict by applying the approaches taught in the earlier classroom portion. Practice is known as a way to master and improve a skill. During the role play, typically the instructor and other students observe and then provide feedback. It all sounds perfectly logical. The catch is, is role play really practice?

Schlegel et al. (2011) conducted a research study on communication skills for health-care professionals working with patients. The researchers started from the position that good patient-centered communication skills improve diagnostic efficiency, lead to better treatment outcomes, and result in a higher level of satisfaction in both the patients and the physician. The researchers had nurses take the same communication skills training for health-care practitioners. Each nurse would take a particular module on one day and then the next day would apply those skills. In the study, twenty-nine nurses practiced in a peer-to-peer role-play situation, and twenty-six nurses practiced in a standard patient care scenario (a real-life situation). The researchers found both groups of nurses felt more confident in using the communication skills after their practice. However, the twenty-six nurses who practiced in the standard patient care situation, as evaluated by supervising nurses in the field, had improved significantly more than the peer-to-peer role-play group.

As of 2019, research papers and doctoral dissertations are being written supporting the effectiveness of role play. It certainly appears there's solid footing for using this practice. However, the manner in which all these research papers and dissertations that support the efficacy of role play are designed is faulty. They all take a topic to be learned and then give the participants a pretest to establish their currently level of mastery. Next, they teach the topic, then have the students practice using role play. Then the participants take a posttest, and voilà, they've all increased their mastery of the subject. However, there's also been a number of research studies conducted like the one by Schlegel et al. (2011) described above where the research design is to have only some of the participants practice with role play, some other participants doing nothing or doing role-play practice, and/or some participants doing some type of an exercise, like a paper and pencil type, or a real-life scenario as examples. In these studies, all the participants' mastery of the subject improves. The researchers typically find that the students who practice with role play improve from pre- to posttest statistically the same or only slightly better than those who do nothing. Those who perform an exercise improve statistically more than those who role-played or did nothing. In my research-supported opinion, role play is little more than a time filler, and that time could be much better spent on real-life exercises. Role play is not quality practice. A phrase I recall is "practice doesn't make perfect; perfect practice makes perfect." And role play at best is very poor-quality practice.

LEARNING PYRAMID

THE LEARNING PYRAMID was adapted from Dale Edgar's Cone of Experience. The Cone of Experience first appeared in Edgar's 1946 book, *Audio-Visual Methods in Teaching*, and in subsequent editions of the book (fig. 2.1). The book was in fact written for pedagogy (K–12); after all, andragogy theory didn't come along for another twenty-plus years, when Malcolm Knowles (1970) proposed that adults and children learn differently. The Cone of Experience developed by Edgar is a visual display depicting a taxonomy of (learning) experiences ranging from direct experience to pure abstraction. The visual was later modified by others and in some cases renamed the learning pyramid, and the experiences or learning methods were then assigned percentages for learning retention (fig. 2.2). In his book Edgar makes no direct references to learning retention.

I read an online article from the *Washington Post* a few years back, based on work by Dr. Daniel Willingham. The article in essence said, according to Dr. Willingham's reasoning, that the learning pyramid was wrong. It was a short article, but it made a few good supported points. At the bottom of the article readers could post their comments. The first comment (by a self-described corporate learning professional) stated how the article took the position that this critique of the learning pyramid was based on the assumption that it was developed for use in pedagogy (K–12). The commenter stated that the learning pyramid was solely developed for andragogy (adult learning) and that the model is backed up with proven data showing knowledge retention rates for adult learners.

The commenter could not be more wrong. This, my friend, is how myths take on a life of their own and live on and on. Even in the face of some convincing evidence, people with no knowledge, or knowledge that they must know they have no evidence for, insist on stating their false opinion. Remember, you are not entitled to your opinion; you are only entitled to state a position that you can support/defend with valid evidence.

No valid research or evidence exists to support any of the percentages that have been attributed to the experiences or learning methods in the visual (fig. 2.2). Nor could percentages of learning retention ever be determined, as this largely depends on what is being learned. For example, if I am trying to teach a new first-year apprentice maintenance person how to tie a particular knot for lifting purposes, an audiovisual presentation or a demonstration is going to be far better than a discussion about tying the knot, even though according to the learning pyramid it should be the other way around. Another aspect is the students themselves. There is plenty of research to support the idea that a topic that is of high relevance to a learner will result in much higher motivation than a topic that has little relevance to the learner (Keller 1987; Wosnitza and Volet 2005; Crowder 2015). Low-motivation students are not going to actively and purposefully engage in discussion or practice, but they likely would be willing to watch a demonstration or audiovisual presentation and thereby retain more of what was being taught. Hopefully some of that instruction would focus on how the topic was relevant so as to build higher motivation.

Learning, unlike arithmetic, is all gray area; there's no black and white. It is filled with contradictions. No one theory or model will work in all situations, and there is no magic pill. That is the way things are in the psychology field, and education is a subset of the psychology discipline. This is why you will find valid support for and criticism of the learning pyramid. The criticism comes from mostly quantitative studies, and these attack the pyramid model as being "technically" false, which, as I have outlined, is true. Obviously the percentages are not accurate or really even meaningful, and there is no research or evidence to support them. As noted, the learning method relative to learning retention depends on the topic that is being learned and on the makeup of the learner's motivation, background knowledge, and experience.

This leads to the supporters (mostly qualitative studies) of the learning pyramid, which point to the basic premise of the pyramid: the more engaged the learner is, the better the retention will be. There is copious research to support that concept. I'm sure you will agree that if you listen to a lecture, you will retain less than if you are actively taking notes while receiving the lecture. That is really the importance of the pyramid and why it has stood the test of time; it attempts to demonstrate various learning methods (experiences) versus their engagement levels, then relates that to learning retention. The research in support of the pyramid demonstrates that knowledgeable, skilled, and experienced teachers can use the pyramid as a guide to help them make the best decisions in instructional design to maximize their students' engagement and, therefore, learning and retention. The catch is this: knowledgeable, skilled, and experienced teachers know of Edgar's work and its strengths and weaknesses, and subsequently when, where, and how to apply it, or at least that is what the supporter's stance is.

Without getting too involved, I'll say that it basically boils down to the notion that the best instructional method for learning is the one that maximizes the learner's engagement. All the methods in the pyramid have been shown by various studies to be better than the others; the key variables are the topic and the learners' characteristics. The learning pyramid is technically false, but a knowledgeable practitioner can use it as a good reference tool.

In the companies I've worked for, the learning pyramid was

contained in the instructional design guidance documents for the learning and development staff. It was to be applied in course design. The application of the learning pyramid came up as a topic of discussion while I was working for one multinational company. Denise, a senior L & D manager with the company, brought the learning pyramid to my attention as she had concerns about its accuracy and application. What we decided, and what I have found works quite well for corporate learning instructional design, was to remove the percentages because they are meaningless. Next we took the triangle and turned it into a rectangle, as it has been shown that no particular range or method on the pyramid is better than any other given the fact the effectiveness of each is topic and learner dependent.

Having a rectangle with the retention percentages removed, the trainer who is developing a course has a solid list of learning methods to consider. The trainer then examines these general methods and considers which ones to use in the instructional design. Within the larger topic being learned, some elements may be better suited to different learning methods. The course designer needs to focus on evaluating which combination of methods will produce the highest level of learner engagement as this will result in the highest levels of learner retention. The danger with trying to use the learning pyramid with the learning retention percentages is that the person designing the course attempts to have all the learning elements use the highest possible retention rate method that he can fit into the course design. This naturally results in poor choices, overall lower learner engagement, and lower learner retention. Success depends upon focusing on which method will get the highest level of learner engagement.

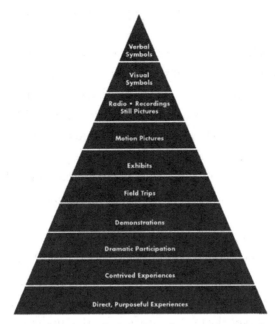

Source: Edgar, Dale. 1946. *Audio-Visual Methods in Teaching.* New York: Dryden Press.

The Learning Pyramid

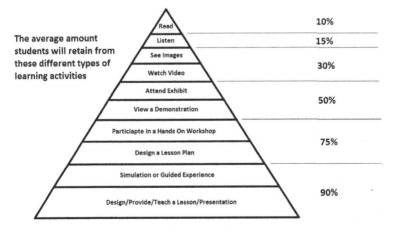

BRAIN-BASED LEARNING

HERE'S ANOTHER TOPIC about which many books have been written, and many of the books define brain-based learning differently. They all try to tie their case back to how the brain works or, more accurately, to the neuroscience of the brain (the biology of how the brain works). As a result, all the books on this subject start from the same premise but then go off in many different directions. I will first explain why the premise itself is faulty. Then I'll debunk some of the more recognized claims of various brain-based learning authors.

Brain-based learning attempts to connect how the brain works physiologically with how it functions cognitively. It wants to take information known on the neuroscience side and make inferences on how it relates to functions on the cognitive side. In the following table, you can see the hierarchy of levels listed under Neuroscience and the hierarchy of levels listed under the Cognitive domain.

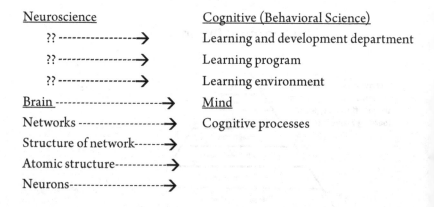

Neuroscience	Cognitive (Behavioral Science)
?? --------------→	Learning and development department
?? --------------→	Learning program
?? --------------→	Learning environment
Brain --------------------→	Mind
Networks --------------------→	Cognitive processes
Structure of network-------→	
Atomic structure-----------→	
Neurons--------------------→	

It takes a lot of work just to figure out on the cognitive side how one level influences the next level up. On the neuroscience side, networks and how they function would relate across the cognitive side to cognitive processes. Just going from one level to the next on either the cognitive or neuroscience side is extremely difficult to do. It is exponentially more difficult to make connections across the two and still have to make another inference up the scale on the cognitive side to gain anything useful. The analogy I like to make is this—it's like examining how a car works and relating it to how it is operated (driven). A heat scan of a car in motion would reveal a large source of heat where the engine is located, and when the car slows down, the four brake rotors would show up as being smaller heat sources than the engine but would be as much as four times hotter. This compares to an MRI or PET scan of the brain during certain brain functions indicating certain areas of the brain are more active than others. With the car, we know the engine and brakes are controlled and operated by the driver, and the driver compartment of the car would show little heat compared to the engine and brakes. Likewise, an MRI scan of the cerebral cortex has shown greater density in people who are fluent in two languages versus just one language. However, just because the cerebral cortex shows the greatest activity during learning doesn't mean a dual-language speaker is a better or a more capable learner. But this is the type of claims brain-based learning makes. Almost all the brain's functions require input from both cerebral hemispheres (Solms and Turnball 2002). Some areas of the brain may be more involved and active than others, but the brain works as one massive interconnected network. You just can't make inferences from neuroscience and apply them to cognitive science (Bruer 1998).

In many of the brain-based learning books I've read, the authors tied Howard Gardner's (1983) multiple intelligence theory, along with learning styles, to support for brain-based learning. Gardner's theory proposes that people have eight separate intelligences: musical, visual, verbal, logical, kinesthetic, interpersonal, intrapersonal, and naturalistic. He later said existential and moral intelligences could be added, making ten in total. His claim is that we have ten intelligences, not one central intelligence as suggested by the intelligence quotient (IQ) theory. Since the multiple intelligence theory was first proposed in 1983, not one of the great number of research studies conducted on this theory has provided any evidence to support the notion that we have multiple intelligences. Conversely, thousands of studies provide evidence and support for IQ theory and show that we have one central intelligence. Even so, a lot of people cling to the multiple intelligence theory, and it is likely popular because it lets us believe that everyone is smart—we just need to determine which of the ten intelligences are highest for someone and then focus their development in that area(s). But it's just not true. We do have abilities. But more on that in chapter 5.

One brain-based learning book I read claimed students need to be physically active while learning. This was based on the fact that the part of the brain that controls physical movement is also responsible for learning. The author offered no source of reference for stating this, of course. As discussed previously, these types of inferences cannot be made. It's like saying that to fill a car with fuel, you need to pump the gas into the engine compartment, not the fuel tank, because the engine compartment is where the fuel gets burned. The same book suggests that the brain does not function in a linear fashion as does organized thought, but rather that it employs multiple strategies to learn. Therefore instruction, it claims, should not be linear. I agree the brain does not learn and process data in a linear manner; however, I've yet to read any research or text on instructional design that finds linear, logical instruction with clear progressions is not the best approach. Can you imagine trying to learn a subject with the instruction jumping all over the place? Just think of the cognitive load that would be placed by trying to keep track, which would clearly take away from understanding the content being taught. Part of the support for nonlinear instruction is based on the claim that the brain can multitask, and therefore step-by-step instructions are not a good approach. No source was cited for the claim that the brain can multitask, and I've found no research to support the claim. I have found plenty of research to the contrary. For example, Cho, Altarriba, and Popiel (2014) found that as the cognitive load increases when multitasking, a person's cognitive performance decreases correspondingly. I think we are all aware of the dangers of distracted driving; humans just cannot multitask very well at all.

I've read about a twelve-principle approach to brain-based learning. You'd be hard-pressed to find any research data supporting the model. The twelve principles suggest things like instructors wearing colored clothing will help learning because of the effect the color has on the brain. You won't find any research connecting the color of clothing to learning, though you will find research that shows part of the brain is stimulated by bright colors, but that hardly makes a case for the claim that colors improve learning. Most brain-based learning writers, it seems, are convinced that learning styles are proven by neuroscience and that learning styles work. However, as described earlier, learning styles do not work. Other claims are that people learn best when they are at the edge of their comfort zones, or that to learn best, the learner must feel safe and secure. Both authors making these differing claims state that their assertions are supported by neuroscience. One of my favorite comments by a brain-based learning author is that brain-based learning focuses on Kirkpatrick's (1998) levels 3 and 4, the highest levels. Really? Because level 2 is the level learning occurs at, not 3 (applying the learning) and not 4 (outcome of applying the learning). Lastly, my favorite of all is from an author who suggested that compelling, personal goals ensure that the amygdala keeps the neocortex switched on. What that means is, the part of the brain that processes emotions and memory keeps the part of the brain that does the higher-level functions (sensory perception, motor control, reasoning, conscious thought, and language) turned on. I mean, it sounds impressive, but it really does not make any sense. Nor do most of the brain-based learning claims that typically come with no cited research sources to back them.

CONCLUSION

AS AN EDUCATOR you need to think critically about what is being advertised to you. We see claims of accelerated learning all the time, claims of how learning time can be shortened and how dollars can be saved if we use a company's new approach to learning styles, or brain-based learning, or the 70-20-10 rule, or microlearning, or company X's software, and so on. Trust me, there are no shortcuts and no magic bullets. Efficient and effective learning comes from doing a thorough needs analysis connected via curriculum to instructional design that suits the topic and audience, delivered with the best approach for the situation, along with embedded instruction that is based on sound principles. It is a lot of work up front on the learning and development end, but it pays off on the learner's end. A good evaluation process will ensure the learning program continually improves and remains current and relevant.

CHAPTER 2

Learner Motivation

INTRODUCTION

THIS CHAPTER EXAMINES learner motivation. A few approaches need to be considered and reflected upon in determining learner motivation. What can be done with instructional design to improve learner motivation? What can the instructor do to create and increase learner motivation? If a learner is motivated enough, she will learn very well, even in spite of poor instructional design or just about any barrier we could put in front of her. By extension, if the instructional design and teaching is of high quality, then a highly motivated student will learn even faster. Counter to this, a student with very low to no motivation will not learn much, if anything, no matter how good the instructional design and teaching is. Of course, high-quality instructional design and teaching will help to create and increase the learner's motivation level.

INTRINSIC AND EXTRINSIC MOTIVATION

INTRINSIC MOTIVATION IS the type of motivation that comes from within us; we are motivated to do something because it's pleasurable for us, and the task or challenge results in a feeling of satisfaction and enjoyment. Extrinsic motivation involves being motivated by something external that provides the learner with the energy to follow through on something in order to receive a reward or avoid a negative consequence. Extrinsic motivation comes from knowing there will be a test and, for example, knowing you need to pass the test as part of your job or to get a job. Intrinsic motivation comes from liking and enjoying the topic being learned. Game theory built into online learning is a way of creating intrinsic motivation in students by making the learning challenging and enjoyable. Generally, intrinsic motivation is considered stronger and longer lasting.

ARCS MODEL

KELLER DEVELOPED AND applied the attention, relevance, confidence, and satisfaction (ARCS) model of motivation for instructional design. The ARCS model provides a method for improving the motivation of students through instruction and the way instructional materials are developed. The model is grounded in expectancy value theory, which works on the principle that people are motivated to engage in an activity if they perceive that it will satisfy a need they have, and the expectation is that the activity will be successful in fulfilling the need. The ARCS model is made up of four conceptual areas, paraphrased from Keller (1987):

1. **Attention** is part of what makes up motivation, and it is a prerequisite for learning. Gaining a student's attention is the first part; the more difficult aspect is having that attention sustained and focused on the appropriate stimuli.

2. **Relevance** is created by having the instruction relate to a problem or potential problem in a learner's life. If the material is perceived as having little or no relevant use for the student, then the instructional design must provide relevance. For example, if a person was just promoted to a supervisory position and now has to use the company's HR software for entering various employee data, he will likely find training on this software very relevant, whereas before becoming a supervisor and not having access to the software, he would have found learning how to use it irrelevant. Another example, but within the instructional design, is that students with a high need for affiliation will enjoy working in groups with other students; this makes the learning relevant to their social needs.

3. **Confidence** has an effect on a student's persistence to accomplish a challenging task. Confident people see ability and effort as leading to success, whereas people with low confidence see luck or difficulty as being the determining factors in success. People with low confidence have an ego influence where they need to impress others. Therefore, this makes them fear failing, rather than simply being focused on working toward success. The students need to feel that if they work reasonably hard at learning a topic, they will be successful at learning it.

4. **Satisfaction** is the positive, good feeling people have when they accomplish something. According to reinforcement theory, people will be motivated if a task and the reward are known. It is important that the reward not be controlled by the teacher but be within the control of the student.

Keller (1987) found that learning following the ACRS model produces true satisfaction within the learner.

ACCELERATED LEARNING

I COULD HAVE talked about accelerated learning in the chapter on myths. As learning and development professionals, we see this term used by all kinds of vendors to describe their products. The only real known method for learning that would truly qualify for the definition of accelerated learning would be Vygotsky's (1978) cognitive development theory.

Vygotsky (1978, 86) describes what he calls a "zone of proximal development." This represents the area between the current level of development a child is at and the level of development a child is capable of being at if his or her developing cognitive functions are brought out with the aid of an adult or more advanced peer. This jump in development can only be made possible through interaction with others who are more developed.

I think the use of mentors and coaches has become pretty commonplace in the work world these days; we have seen this approach with apprenticeship programs since before Vygotsky proved the case in his research. In most cases with adults, the mentor or coach is nothing more than a good learning aid for the learner, but on accession the jump is made possible only by the aid of someone more advanced. In 1954 Robert Bannister did what no one believed was possible—he ran the mile in less than four minutes. Many believed the human body was physically incapable of running a mile in less than four minutes, and they believed that if anyone were to do so, that person would collapse and die of exhaustion. Once Bannister proved it could be done, within a year, thirty-six other people had run the mile in less than four minutes. Having the confidence in knowing something was possible made all the difference to the other runners. The confidence in learning, to know and deeply believe you can accomplish/learn something as demonstrated by someone else (a more advanced peer), can make all the difference.

RELEVANCE AND SELF-EFFICACY

EMOTIONAL AND SOCIAL dimensions related to learning do have an influence on a student's learning, according to Wosnitza and Volet (2005); in their study they examined the impact of emotions on learning. Their study determined that the topic to be learned could be perceived as anywhere in the range from familiar and easy to unfamiliar and difficult. Regardless of where on the spectrum the course was perceived to be, if the topic was also perceived to be relevant to the learner's personal goals, the generated emotion would result in an emotional arousal that resulted in the person's motivation to pursue the learning. This fits with Keller's ARCS model (1987), where relevance relates to providing the learner with a positive benefit in terms of fulfilling a need for her that is also found to be a motivating force.

Bandura (1982, 1997) developed social cognitive theory, which predicts that a person is more likely to behave or do a certain thing if he or she fully expects that it will deliver positive benefits. Relevance is a central component; an individual needs to recognize a different behavior as being beneficial for him, rather than unrewarding for him, before he will make a change.

A student's positive self-efficacy correlates strongly to higher academic results in learning. This is confirmed by the research of Artino (2010), Lynch (2003), and Wang and Newlin (2002). Self-efficacy is the confidence level a person feels about his or her ability to accomplish a specified task. High self-efficacy enables people to stick to their goals in the face of obstacles. The higher a student's self-efficacy, the greater the chances are of his or her success in mastering a change in behavior (Brehm 2004). A person's self-efficacy can be increased through helping him or her see early results from the behavior change. Providing the education enables the person to know he or she is on the correct path, which will subsequently also provide positive reinforcement (McAuley and Blissmer 2000; Schilcht, Godin, and Camaione 1999).

Cognitive processes are different strategies learners will employ to aid them in learning a new task or material. Task value for a student can be described as the degree to which he or she finds a task important and/or useful (Artino and Stephens 2006). Task value then can be seen as similar to relevance for a learner. Artino and Stephens (2006) found that when students felt a learning topic had high task value for them, and when they themselves also had high self-efficacy for learning, it was a strong predictor that those students would report using the cognitive processes of elaboration, critical thinking, and metacognitive strategies in learning the topic. This supports the idea that relevance and self-efficacy, which are elements of motivation, are linked with academic (learning) performance.

Elaboration, critical thinking, and metacognitive strategies can fit under a larger category of self-regulated learning. Self-regulation is a process through which learners "set their own goals and manage their own learning performance" (Driscoll 2000, 304). This self-regulatory process is a cycle with three stages. Stage 1, forethought, occurs when the learner makes plans and establishes goals for the learning. Stage 2, performance control, occurs when the student exercises self-regulation for effort and concentration during the learning. Stage 3, self-reflection, occurs when the learner reflects on what was learned and evaluates its usefulness, which in turn affects future forethought, thereby completing the cycle (Zimmerman 1990).

Self-regulated learning strategies are the processes learners use to aid themselves in learning. These can be broken down into various types of strategies as described by Haihong and Gramling (2009, 127–28):

- ➢ Metacognition
  - Goal setting: determining target results of learning, and setting subgoals
  - Strategic planning: deciding on learning methods to achieve goals
  - Self-monitoring: keeping track of behavior, cognition, and motivation
  - Self-evaluation: making judgments and causal attribution of performance
  - Cognitive rehearsal: selecting and encoding information in a verbatim manner
  - Organization: making internal connections from the information in the learning
  - Elaboration: connecting learning material with material found from other sources and past knowledge

- ➢ Resource Management
  - Time management: scheduling, planning, coordinating one's time
  - Environment: organizing the study environment to be efficient and free of distractions

- Effort regulation: controlling effort and attention in the face of distractions and uninteresting tasks
- Help seeking: obtaining help from others to overcome academic difficulties

The use of self-regulatory learning strategies has been found to result in more positive learner motivation (Schunk and Ertmer 1999; Zimmerman and Kitsantas 1999), greater persistence (Lan 1996), and higher academic (learning) achievement (Schunk and Swartz 1993; Zimmerman and Martinez-Pons 1986).

In one of my research studies (Crowder 2015), I examined learners' motivation and compared that to their success in learning the given topic. Twenty-seven elite athletes were supplied with sports nutrition mobile learning that they could access with their smartphones, tablets, or laptops. In this learning experiment, I found there was a strong correlation between learning success and relevance. The more the athletes felt the nutritional learning could help them be more successful athletes, the greater their learning. While self-efficacy was examined, it did not play nearly as dominant a role as relevance did in motivating the learners to overcome obstacles and put in the effort and have the determination required to learn. The instructional design incorporated a short video at the very beginning that focused on describing sports nutrition in a manner that relayed how it was relevant for these athletes.

I strongly believe that for all courses, it is vital to establish and help the potential students see the relevance of the learning. It is of the utmost importance to know what makes the learning topic relevant to the learners and then to make sure they know the course addresses that relevant need. This builds learner interest and motivation. I try to incorporate how a topic is relevant into advanced information or the advertising of a course as well. The more relevant the students find the learning, the greater their motivation, and consequently the greater your success will be in having them master the learning. This results in both the instructor and the student reaping the benefits.

The Workplace Hazardous Materials Information System (WHMIS) is government-mandated training in Canada for employees who work with hazardous materials. There is a large number of safety companies that provide the necessary training. In order to make this training the most relevant, examples used in the course should be the hazardous materials a particular company uses. Safety companies who supply this training typically choose common recognizable hazardous materials for their course examples. For this type of training I prefer to build the course in-house or else work with a vendor to modify the material so it is specific to the hazardous material(s) our people are actually working with. The more relevant the training material can be, the better success you can expect from the learners.

MOBILE LEARNING RESEARCH EXAMPLE

MOBILE LEARNING, OR m-learning, is learning that takes place anywhere, anytime, by use of a handheld internet-connected technology, for example smartphones, tablets, or laptop computers. Shih and Mills (2007) introduced mobile learning into an established literature class. The researchers were interested to find out how mobile technologies influence teaching and learning in a traditional education setting. They evaluated the students' learning and considered the benefits and challenges of using mobile learning in this situation. Their research showed mobile learning with its 24/7 access and its capacity to allow the learner to learn "anywhere, anytime" can support independent and collaborative learning. Mobile learning helps students to recognize areas where they need help and also helps to reduce the formality of the class atmosphere. The increased awareness of the students, coupled with the reduced formality, helps to engage the reluctant learner. Most significantly, Shih and Mills found that mobile learning helps learners stay engaged in the learning for longer periods of time, and mobile learning helps to raise students' self-esteem and self-confidence.

In constructing their model, Shih and Mills (2007) followed Keller's ARCS model of motivational design. The first phase of the ARCS model is to create interest within the learners. The second phase is to demonstrate how the learning will be of relevance to the learners. The third phase creates a situation where the learners can gain confidence with the learning, and the fourth and final phase provides a situation where the learners can apply their new learning in a real or simulated situation. The experiment by Shih and Mills was conducted at California State University with forty-six students. The students were allowed to access the course contents at their Moodle website using smartphones. In addition to this, learning notifications were sent by text message. The students were able to join other students in online discussions, and learning activities were completed electronically. The aim of this experiment was to give students the added convenience and flexibility to complete the course requirements.

Shih and Mills (2007) adapted the ARCS learning model to mobile technology in order to create Shih's mobile-learning model. For the attention aspect of Keller's model, Shih and Mills sent a multimedia message to the students' mobile phones to act as a reminder and motivate the students. For the relevance aspect, the researchers then sent a message containing embedded hyperlinks with related information. They added a combination step where both the relevance and the confidence aspects were addressed, incorporating peer-to-peer discussion using text, voice, images, and video. The learners then produced a digital story in either audio or video format. Lastly, for the satisfaction component of Keller's model, Shih and Mills (2007) had the students apply their learning in an online simulated environment, producing an educational game. A summary of the findings by Shih and Mills include the following:

- students appreciated the added flexibility that m-learning provided;
- students had higher levels of motivation;
- there was an improvement in the interaction between students and with the instructor;
- students found this type of instruction attractive;
- the students were more willing to collaborate; and
- the quality of learning was determined to be as good as or better than the traditional face-to-face classroom delivery of the course.

Shih and Mills (2007) also felt that Vygotsky's (1978) cognitive development theory fit well with mobile learning. Through the "zone of proximal development," a jump in development can occur. This jump in development can only be made possible through interaction with others who are more developed. Mobile learning allows for a learner to be connected to a person more developed in the specific area, which, according to Vygotsky, enables them to learn more than they otherwise could on their own. While this connection to other, more capable people can be the case for other types of learning, with mobile learning the connection can be made anywhere, anytime, thereby enhancing the learner's opportunity for this to happen.

WEBSITE RESEARCH EXAMPLE

I LIKE THIS research study because it deals with nonformal learning, namely, a situation where you need to get the learner's attention and keep it. From this type of nonformal learning, I think we can glean very valuable lessons on how to get a learner motivated and how maintain that motivation. Lin and Gregor (2006) looked at websites designed for learning and enjoyment. The researchers chose to examine museum websites. The websites chosen had been created to support the respective museum's mission of providing the public with educational material for study and enjoyment. These websites are designed not as part of any formal education undertaking but rather to provide enjoyment to the user while learning. This exploratory study conducted a number of semistructured interviews with both museum and educational experts. The interviews lasted on average one and a half hours. The major questions asked are summarized as follows:

1. What have your experiences been with e-learning websites in your organization?
2. Do you think that an e-learning website can encourage learning for the general public? If yes, how? If no, why not?
3. What are the conditions for creating an enjoyable learning experience with an e-learning website?
4. How can a website for the enjoyment of e-learning be developed?

The article provides a short overview of e-learning and provides the two characteristics that define e-learning according to the Australian National Training Authority. First, it is assisted by information and communication technologies, and second, diverse media is required for e-learning to be effective. The experts interviewed by Lin and Gregor added that the use of interactivity and multimedia helped to capture the learner's attention and improved his or her learning experience. The article provides a discussion of what enjoyment is and then comes to the conclusion that enjoyment simply means the meeting and fulfillment of one's needs, or simply to fulfill what a person is motivated to learn. The paper then explores what the needs are, examining the human motivation work of Maslow (1987) and Ford (1992), which leads to the goals humans have. These include affective, cognitive, subjective organization, self-assertive social relationship, integrative social relationship, and task goals. We are predisposed to achieving these goals. Learning can satisfy a number of our needs or goals; therefore, it can be enjoyable as long as there is a positive effect to it. This enjoyment stems from intrinsically motivated learning. The paper's conclusion is that effective learning websites need to be enjoyable, supportive, positive, active, engaging, contextual, and collaborative. To achieve this, six features were determined:

1. The website needs to be aesthetically pleasing.
2. It needs to have interaction with the learners.
3. It needs to be easy to use. The learner should find it easy to navigate and should find it trouble-free.
4. The learner should have the flexibility to learn using the method that he or she wants, and when he or she wants, reflecting that it should be asynchronous.
5. The learning tasks should be short and without any testing as the experience should be relaxing for the learner.
6. Useful hyperlinks should be part of the website.

The paper also proposed four development guidelines: multimedia and interactive technology; solid characteristics of adult learning; the provision of adequate funding and qualified personnel for the website; and the fact that it needs to take into consideration who the target audience will be. A final guideline is to build the website to sharable course object reference model (SCORM) standards to enable the information to be more sharable.

CONCLUSION

IF STUDENTS FIND the topic to be learned relevant, they will be intrinsically motivated to pursue and master the learning. The greater the relevance, the stronger the motivation. Most workplaces will have extrinsic motivators, such as the learning is required for a job or by the company or a regulatory body. Extrinsic motivators are typically out of the control of the learner or the learning and development group. However, the element that has the strongest effect on motivation is relevance. The learning and development professional needs to leverage this knowledge to maximize his or her students' motivation. Incorporating the principles of the ARCS model, and by extension other related strategies like game theory, will support and strengthen the student's motivation.

CHAPTER 3

Learning Theories

INTRODUCTION

LEARNING CAN BE defined as gaining actionable knowledge (Siemens 2005). Unlike science where we rely on one theory that will explain one or more phenomena, like Newton's theory of gravitation, which explains gravitational attraction, there is no one single learning theory that covers how all learning is accomplished. There are over fifty known published accepted learning theories. Many of the theories overlap, and certainly any teaching or course design involves multiple learning theories. In this chapter I begin by describing some of these theories, starting with the basic most widely used theories, then move on to more complex learning theories that in some cases encompass aspects of other, simpler learning theories. A very large book could easily be written on this topic. I have chosen to write briefly on the learning theories that are common and applicable to workplace learning and development.

BEHAVIORISM LEARNING THEORY

THE BASIC PREMISE of behaviorism theory, which came about in the 1930s, is that a learner's behavior is shaped by responding to environmental stimuli. The stimuli come in the form of positive or negative reinforcement. A person is more likely to adopt a new behavior if pleasurable consequences are experienced as a result of the new behavior (Skinner 1953). Negative reinforcement works by providing the learner with something unpleasurable when the desired behavior is not exhibited. Conversely, positive reinforcement could be withheld if the desired behavior is not performed; or by performing as desired, the learner can avoid negative reinforcement. At the risk of being overly simplistic, I ask you to think of teaching a dog to use the backyard as its toilet instead of the floors in the house. If the dog does its business outside, it is given praise and a treat. If the dog does it on the floor in the house, it gets scolded and receives a spanking. That's the basic idea of behaviorism learning theory. It's more complicated with people; in training courses, the approach is basically applied by rewarding the desired behavior and punishing the unwanted behavior. For example, an instructor lets the class know that if they return to the training session on time after breaks and stay focused, they will be rewarded with the course ending sooner, thereby allowing them to leave for home earlier. If they do not, then the class will run later. Another use of this theory is acknowledging students by way of a positive comment for their contributions to class discussions.

COGNITIVISM LEARNING THEORY

COGNITIVISM GAINED TRACTION in the 1950s. Behaviorism has its merits, but as cognitivism suggests, people are much more than programmed beings. The basic premise of this theory is that as learning comes to the person, he processes the content, and based on that thought process, he acts as a result, and his behavior is an outcome. The focus of cognitivism learning theory is based on how the brain does things. How does the brain process, store, and retrieve information? How does it solve problems? Cognitivism aims to better understand these processes to help the learner. Take a simple example: we know the brain remembers things better if they are repeated, so we make sure there is repetition in our lessons. It is out of this theory that brain-based learning comes, but as I discussed in the chapter on myths, the proponents have strayed too far.

CONSTRUCTIVISM LEARNING THEORY

THE CONSTRUCTIVISM THEORY comes from the work of Jean Piaget (1896–1980). The concept of constructivism is that learners construct new knowledge themselves. The learner does not learn what the teacher is teaching per se. The learner takes the information coming from the teacher and integrates it with past experiences, knowledge, and current ideas to form new knowledge. For example, if a learner is being taught how to tie a reef knot, she'll likely construct the knowledge that the first part of the knot is exactly the same as the first part of tying her shoes. She takes new information and combines it with past experiences to learn or construct new knowledge. The biomechanics of tying the knot will also be accomplished by having the experience of handling and using ropes and laces in the past.

HUMANISM LEARNING THEORY

EARLY IN THE nineteenth century, theologian Friedrich Niethammer used the term *humanism* to describe a person-centered educational approach that takes into account the entire person as a whole; it considers higher-order concepts of freedom, human potential, and dignity. The idea is that people's actions are based on their values. The student is not simply taught strictly a subject, but rather the student as a whole person is taught. This requires enabling the student to be part of the process and giving him the ability to make choices about the learning process. It requires the instructor to be empathetic toward the students and to genuinely care about them as people, not just their learning of a particular subject.

I think (I hope) most of us experienced a humanistic approach in K–12 school, whereas in first-year university with two hundred students in a lecture hall, and with a professor who cared much more about his or her research work than about students—well, it was not so humanistic an approach. In the workplace there is a strong humanistic influence; typically the courses employees take are focused on the employees' development. The employees in many cases have options such as what dates to take the course, and during the course they have some say over break times and the like. You will be able to make more inferences on the humanistic approach after reading the chapter on ethics.

Speaking of ethics and humanism, I wonder about my parents' stories of the Catholic nuns who taught K–12 back in the first half of the twentieth century. The stories go that any disobedience was met with a crack of the yardstick over their backs. I'm sure the nuns fully believed at the time that this discipline was in the children's best developmental interests (as did most parents who used corporal punishment back then), so was it a humanistic approach or not?

GESTALT LEARNING THEORY

GESTALT IS FROM the German language. It does not have a direct translation into English, but it roughly means organization, pattern, or configuration. Gestalt psychology sees learning as more complicated for humans than the simplicity of reward and punishment with the learning focus on subparts of a larger topic. The concept of gestalt is that we do not learn by the parts, but rather we learn the whole of something by recognizing patterns and forming relationships from knowledge of our past experiences and using this to construct the learning of the whole. For instance, when we see a car drive by, we see a car, the whole; we don't typically see thousands of little parts all stuck together moving down the road. I recently saw pictures of a car that had folding wings such that the car could drive on public roads but then go to an airstrip and, with the wings mechanically extended and a rear prop engaged to the engine, fly as it became an airplane. By using my previous knowledge and recognizing what makes up a car and what makes up an airplane, I quickly learned the vehicle was both a plane and car, even though I had never seen one before. This link between previous experience and learning is seen in other learning theories.

Gestalt theory extends to problem-solving in that we examine the whole problem. Take for example the following problem:

$$1 + 4 = 5$$
$$2 + 5 = 12$$
$$3 + 6 = 21$$
$$8 + 11 = ?$$

If the problem solver were to just focus on the final line of the problem with the question mark, she would say the answer is 19. But by solving the problem as a whole, as gestalt theory suggests we do, she would determine the answer by adding up the horizontal line plus the result of the previous vertical line, or 8 + 11 + 21, which gives the problem's solution of 40.

ADULT LEARNING THEORY (ANDRAGOGY)

IN THEIR EIGHTH edition of *The Adult Learner*, Knowles, Holton, and Swanson (2015) explain the theory of adult learning, which Knowles refers to as *andragogy* in his book *The Adult Learner: A Neglected Species* (1978). From the theory, the authors describe characteristics of adult learners and explain how to enable and support adult learners. The basis for the andragogy learning theory rests on the following six assumptions of adult learners, paraphrased from Knowles, Holton, and Swanson:

1. **The need to know.** Adult learners need to know why they need to learn something before undertaking to learn it.
2. **Learner self-concept.** Adults need to be responsible for their own decisions and to be treated as capable of self-direction.
3. **Role of learners' experience.** Adult learners have a variety of experiences in life that represent the richest resource for learning.
    These experiences are, however, imbued with bias and presupposition.
4. **Readiness to learn.** Adults are ready to learn those things they need to know in order to cope effectively with life situations.
5. **Orientation to learning.** Adults are life-centered (or task-centered or problem-centered) as pertains to learning. Adults are motivated to learn in order to perform tasks or deal with problems or situations in their lives.

6. **Motivation.** While adults do respond to some external (extrinsic) motivators such as higher pay, job promotion, or a better job, the most powerful motivators for adults are intrinsic or internal pressures such as better quality of life, increased job satisfaction, and higher self-esteem.

For learning to be effective, adult learners need to determine their own learning objectives, such that the learning objectives will then be relevant to their self-determined needs. In most cases, workers see learning as something that will help them perform their jobs better or to meet the compliance requirements of their jobs. As a result, the workers perceive the learning as relevant to their needs. Adult learners prefer to be self-directed in learning. Knowles, Holton, and Swanson (2015) believe children progressively move toward self-directedness in their learning as they age and mature. The authors provide direction for engaging, motivating, implementing, and evaluating when teaching adults. Knowles (1989) foresaw technology as being beneficial in supporting self-directed learning, saying it could provide just-in-time learning with the learner being in complete control. *The Adult Learner* points out that evidence is growing to support the idea that when adults are self-directed in learning, the learning is deeper and more permanent than when adults learn by being directed by another person.

STUDENT-CENTERED LEARNING THEORY

THE STUDENT-CENTERED APPROACH is consistent with Knowles's adult learning theory. Hannafin, Hannafin, and Gabbitas (2009) studied student-centered Web-based learning. The authors note that in student-centered learning, learners take on the responsibility of setting their learning goals and tracking their progress, as well as making changes and adapting those goals as needed. The learners make the determination for when their goals are met. Mickelson, Kaplan, and MacNeily (2009) created a student-centered curriculum that resulted in an active learning outcome. As a result of a mandate from the Royal Canadian College of Physicians and Surgeons, the University of British Columbia (UBC) urologic curriculum needed to be changed. A curriculum committee was formed, comprised of three final-year resident students and the program director. The committee shifted from the traditional "active teacher, passive student" approach to a more student-centered learning approach for the new curriculum. Weekly topics for learning were chosen with a resident expert appointed to lead the week's article reviews and discussions. Third-year to fifth-year residents were responsible for delivering different topics on the curriculum to their fellow residents and had the responsibility for testing the others on the topic. For certain competencies that were required to be addressed (e.g., the financial planning competency, which is part of the physician manager component), guest speakers were brought in.

Observations the authors made on the new approach were that the resident students supported the curriculum and took ownership. The residents presented material that they wanted to learn more about and became experts in it. It was observed that there was a shift in the learning, namely that the students adopted an active learning approach to the new curriculum. Active learning is defined as a metacognitive process, the ability of the learner to monitor his or her current levels of understanding and develop an idea of how he or she learns. During active learning, students take responsibility for their learning. In conclusion, the shift in pedagogy from an approach of having an active teacher and passive students to a constructivist approach of having the curriculum student-centered led to the unforeseen creation of an active learning environment that proved to be positive, with student satisfaction and buy-in. The active learning produced a successful outcome resulting in deep learning, motivated learners, and a student-directed curriculum.

CONNECTIVISM LEARNING THEORY

SIEMENS (2005) PROPOSED the learning theory connectivism. Technology has changed the way people work and function in the world. Connectivism is a model of learning for a society where learning has evolved from being strictly an internal individual activity.

Behaviorism, cognitivism, and constructivism learning theories were developed years before learning was impacted by technology. It was a time when the half-life of knowledge was measured in decades, whereas today, knowledge in the world is doubling in less than two years. Behaviorism, cognitivism, and constructivism learning theories addressed how a person learns. Connectivism takes its roots from objectivism, pragmatism, and interpretivism learning theories, which consider knowledge to be an objective or state that is reached through reasoning and/or experiences. These theories take the position that learning occurs outside the person, whereas in behaviorism, cognitivism, and constructivism learning theories, the concept is that learning is internal. Connectivism is best described as networks made up of nodes with each node representing a learning community. Learning communities are groups that share interests and interact with each other by sharing knowledge, ideas, and thinking. A change in one node can have a ripple effect, creating change across the network. Siemens (2005) stated that the principles of connectivism are these:

- Learning and knowledge rest in a diversity of opinions.
- Learning is a process of connecting specialized nodes or information sources.
- Learning may reside in nonhuman appliances.
- The capacity to know more is more critical than what is currently known.
- Nurturing and maintaining connections is needed to facilitate continual learning.
- The ability to see connections between fields, ideas, and concepts is a core skill.
- Accurate, up-to-date knowledge is the intent of all connectivist learning activities.
- Decision-making is in itself a learning process, and choosing what to learn and the meaning of incoming information is seen through the lens of shifting reality (what's right today may be wrong tomorrow because of changes in information).

Here's an example of how this theory plays out in the real world: Let's say you bought an old, worn-out all-terrain vehicle (ATV). It's so worn out that it doesn't even run, and you've never owned or even driven one before. You bought it at a garage sale for $10—how could you pass up such a bargain? Besides, you have always wanted one. How would you go about learning how to fix it up and where to get parts? The internet would probably be your first step. You would likely join a discussion forum and read and ask questions of those who are very knowledgeable about the workings of an ATV, where to get parts for older ones, and so on. From there you would contact those parts dealers, and maybe you would find a good one locally and go talk to them. What you would be doing is creating a network. You would learn from this network. Eventually you would rebuild the ATV and become very knowledgeable, at which point you would begin sharing knowledge with others in the network. At some point a new product may come to the market that makes something on most or all ATVs outdated; this would be a ripple through the network. If you're thinking this is based on a true story of my experience, well, you're sort of right, only it were an old race car and not an ATV. And unfortunately it wasn't a $10 bargain.

Another example or thought is to consider how a nuclear energy plant would go from being approved to being completely built. No one person has all the knowledge required to build it. There's the engineering for the construction, which involves multiple engineering disciplines, so no one engineer would know everything involved in the design. Within the construction there are multiple specialized trades and equipment, and computerized controls that contain thousands of lines of software code. There's the coordination of thousands of workers to build the plant. And so on. If you think about it, connectivism is what allows it to all happen effectively and efficiently.

CONCLUSION

THIS CHAPTER ONLY covers a handful of the learning theories out there. These are the most commonly known and applied learning theories. It would take an entire to book to do even a brief review of all the learning theories. Which learning theory or theories to apply depends on a number of aspects: the students, the instructional design, the learning environment, and the content, to name just a few. Instructional designers and instructors who are well versed in the various theories will recognize, based on the variables of the situation, which learning theory or combination of theories is best to apply. For example, if you were to have a new employee come into your learning group and she needed to use your company's learning management software, you would teach different functions using several examples, not just showing them once. This would be cognitivism learning theory at work. You would provide feedback while the employee attempted to perform functions with the software herself. This would be the application behaviorism learning theory. Once she was working on her own, you would provide support by answering any emailed questions she might have. This would be connectivism at work.

CHAPTER 4

Crowder's Mastery Theory

HOWARD GARDNER'S THEORY of multiple intelligences (1983) has generated a large following. His theory originally proposed that people have more than one intelligence; he suggested we all have eight intelligences: musical (rhythmic), logical (mathematical), bodily (kinesthetic), interpersonal, intrapersonal, naturalistic, visual (spatial), and verbal (linguistic). Furthermore, an individual could be high in one intelligence and low in another. The theory makes a lot of sense. Most educators could offer anecdotal evidence that seems to bear out the idea that the theory has some validity. However, research since the theory came out in 1983 has pretty much shown that people have only one central intelligence, referred to as intelligence quotient (IQ).

Still, what explains how a person can be good at one thing and not very good at another? Is it simply a result of the amount of work and effort? Perhaps because we had bad experiences learning in a particular area early on in life, we've concluded that we're not good at that area of study; as a result, we never really worked hard in the area again, thereby creating a self-fulfilling prophecy. Perhaps, but I think Gardner was on to something.

Take for example Ernest Rutherford, born in 1871. He went on to win a Nobel Prize in 1908 for his work in the field of radioactive substances. Rutherford was not considered very bright by his peers, he was considered to be quite weak at mathematics, and he was not particularly creative with the design of experiments. He was, however, brilliant at physics. Also important to note is that Rutherford was considered to be one of the most determined, hardworking, and tenacious scientists of his time (Bryson 2004). What could explain Rutherford's being brilliant at physics and subpar at math and experimentation if he had only one central intelligence?

I propose that individuals have a number of abilities that are driven by their IQ. These abilities are not like the intelligences Gardner proposed, and I highly doubt these abilities would neatly fit into categories humankind has already created and defined, such as musical or mathematical intelligence. These abilities are likely very abstract. I would suggest we have a great number of these abstract abilities that work in combination to allow us to make use of skills as complex as math and music. Each one of these numerous abilities can range from low to high or fall anywhere in between.

A teacher who has taught high school math for twenty-five years will tell you that over that time, no two students have had the exact same aptitude at math. No surprise, because as we all know, no two humans are the same. If IQ is our only intelligence, and if 99 percent of the population falls between 80 and 150 on the IQ scale, well, you can see that millions of people are going to have very close to the same IQ. I believe the differentiators are our abilities. For example, if our skill in math is a result of the combination of, say, eight, twenty-two, or more abstract abilities that each have their own levels that are then leveraged by our IQ, then now we can see the odds are less likely that two people have the same math aptitude. For example, no two people have the same handwriting, and police handwriting experts can tell the differences between the original and a very good forgery. We learn to handwrite at an early age, and we are shown examples of what the outcome should look like. Our handwriting is then the result of our IQ driving our abilities (of various levels) that make up our physical hand muscle coordination and our artistic abilities, coupled with how we perceive what we are trying to write and what we have drawn, and finally how hard and how long we work at perfecting our technique. The result is not just the shapes drawn but also the pressure applied to the writing instrument in doing so. It is the abilities and effort applied that result in the difference(s).

Besides having a central IQ driver and central abilities, there's the influence of the amount of effort and work that is applied. As the saying goes, perfect practice makes perfect. The more effort and work, the greater the result—to a point. For example, in sports it takes ten thousand hours of dedicated practice for a person to reach their potential (Gladwell 2008); after the ten thousand hours, the practice and work is continued in order to maintain that level, and any improvement is no longer significant. It's not just ten thousand hours either, as it's unlikely any two athletes would practice and work through that ten thousand hours with the same intensity and drive or with the same response to injuries and other setbacks throughout the journey.

The same goes for students learning math, science, music, and so on. To illustrate the impact of determination, work, and effort, I offer this story: In college I needed a 70 percent final grade in a first-year math course. The final exam was worth 40 percent, and my average going in was 64 percent, meaning I needed at least 82 percent, a higher mark by far than what I'd achieved on any test, including the two midterm exams. My marks were all in the 60 percent to 70 percent range over two semesters, with the same professor for both semesters. I scored 94 percent on the final. I remember the professor calling me into his office afterward as the mark difference was cause for concern—possible cheating, I suppose. The professor said he was fairly certain I did not cheat, but he wanted to understand how this was possible. I explained, to his dismay, that every test and exam we had was held during the first period on Thursdays and that on every Wednesday evening before every one of those tests and exams, there was a Toronto Maple Leafs hockey game broadcast on television. Being good Canadian boys, I and a group of friends had a tradition of sorts where we would get together to have a few beers and watch the hockey game. This left me no time to study for any of this professor's math tests or exams. But, I explained, the Leafs had been eliminated from the playoffs two weeks before the final exam, so I actually studied for it, hence the 94 percent. I still remember the look on his face; obviously he was not a big hockey fan. Throughout the semester my IQ and ability level had not changed, but my determination and resulting effort and work did change, resulting in a far different outcome. I think we've all seen and experienced this ourselves; determination can make a large impact on learning or mastery success.

The effort, intensity, hours, and dedication a person puts into learning and mastering anything can be defined by his or her level of determination. A person's level of determination is created by his or her interest in succeeding in the given area. That interest is driven by the relevance that succeeding has to the individual (Crowder 2015). It may be relevant for a person to satisfy his or her ego or for a child to satisfy his or her parents, or it could truly be an intrinsic source of interest likely triggered by an early unremembered experience that produced a positive feeling or connection to the area they have this interest to succeed in.

I recently read a book by Timothy Caufield (2012) in which he explains that while growing up, he was always the fastest runner in his class right up through high school. He was a very good sprinter. He was always on his school's track team and as a result put in many hours of dedicated training for sprinting. Part of writing his book involved getting a genetic test. These tests look at a person's genetic makeup, for instance, examining the percentage of slow-twitch muscle fiber to fast-twitch muscle fiber. The test results are then interpreted to determine which sports that person would be best suited for. Mr. Caufield was surprised when the results came back stating he would not be any good at sprinting because he did not have the genetic makeup for it. He wondered how that could possibly be. My theory would suggest his IQ was driving high abilities in the area of the muscle coordination involved in sprinting. At a young age in a small group of peers, he was likely the fastest, which provided him with satisfaction and confidence and, over the years, led to him putting in a great deal of intense practice, resulting in his becoming a very good sprinter. My theory suggests from this example that with above-average abilities in a particular area and determined sustained work, a high level of success can be achieved, despite not having the best genetic makeup.

On a 2016 *60 Minutes* telecast, Neil deGrasse Tyson, a world-famous astrophysicist, explained that when he was in grade school, his teachers pushed him toward athletics, presumably because he was black. He felt it was likely a cultural bias of the day as blacks were seen to be good athletes. Neil had to choose the path of most resistance in order to pursue science. Inside he knew he liked science and had an aptitude (the ability) for it. Obviously, he also has a high IQ leveraging his abilities. I think most of all, Neil knew he had the determination to put in the effort and work to be successful in science.

My theory can be articulated as follows:

Success in learning (mastering) a topic = IQ × Abilities × Determination

When it is laid out this way, we can see that a person with a low IQ but with strong abilities (for the given area) and high determination would be quite successful and would outperform a person with high IQ, average ability levels, and low determination. As instructors, teachers, and coaches, we've all had those experiences where a person with seemingly low aptitude in a particular area who puts in a great deal of sustained work and effort becomes very proficient in the given area. For each person, IQ is a constant (k), and for 95 percent of the population the difference in IQ is not very great. A person's abilities are also a constant for them, but the combination of abilities in different areas can make a substantial difference as some abilities may be high and others lower. Determination is a variable that can make a huge difference as effort will vary with the amount of determination.

The majority of people have an IQ that falls into the average range, and an average of all these abstract abilities for most of these people would also average out to being somewhere in the middle. But with all these abstract abilities, some will combine for us to be above average in some areas and below average in others. Of course, there are people like Stephen Hawking, Wayne Gretzky, and Albert Einstein whose abilities in certain areas are off-the-charts high. I'd guess they would score above average in IQ as well, but sadly we don't all get those genes. But I digress. The key to success is finding out which ability areas we are above average in, which can be difficult to know for certain, as the Timothy Caufield sprinter example demonstrates.

The other key is to know which areas where we have, or

would have, the determination and drive to put in a great deal of intense prolonged effort and work. I would recommend pursuing an area you know you have the determination to pursue. If you have the determination to pursue something more intensely than other things, that thing likely brings you more satisfaction and enjoyment, which contributes to your being happy. In my theory, IQ is essentially irrelevant because it doesn't matter what is pursued as the IQ influence is a constant. Choosing different abilities is an option, but pursuing an area of high ability without high determination won't yield great results. Ideally you have determination for pursing an area in which you have high abilities. In most cases, at a very young age a person will have positive experiences in her areas of high ability, and this will lead to her gaining satisfaction and enjoyment from overcoming challenges and being successful in those areas. In most cases, the areas in which you have high levels of drive and determination are going to be the same areas in which your abilities are higher. While this may not always be the case, as I stated earlier, pursuing an area for which a person has a high level of determination will bring satisfaction and enjoyment. It will also bring success. It's never going to be a bad thing for an individual to pursue an area in which he has a high level of determination to succeed.

I grew up with a guy who loved sports; he practiced hard and had a great attitude. I cannot say for sure, but my impression was that he was of average intelligence, maybe a little above average. He was a dedicated, hardworking student. Like a lot of young boys, he dreamed of being a professional athlete when he grew up. However, this lad was obviously low on the combination of abilities that one would need to be an elite athlete. I am sure he realized earlier than most young boys that earning a living as an athlete was not in his future. However, his love of sports never died, and he went on to become a very successful doctor specializing in the field of sports medicine. I understand he even worked with a professional sports team. He stayed involved with his love of sports in a different way. There is little doubt his determination that drove him to be successful in pursuing a medical degree (no small feat) in large part came from his love of sports and wanting to make a living out of being involved in sports, even though his athletic abilities prevented him from performing sports himself at an elite level.

For the learning and development professional, the question becomes, what does this theory mean in practical terms, and how can you apply it? The variable in the equation is determination, the amount of work and effort a person will put forth in pursuing what you're teaching. Increasing a student's motivation is the key, as it is really the only thing we can influence. The unknown in the equation is what abilities the person has that will combine to create a high-aptitude area for that individual. With IQ there's testing, but for abilities there is no test. It takes observation and honest personal reflection. There are aptitude tests as well. Certainly the most success will be achieved in the area(s) in which a person has the highest level of abilities, provided the person has the drive and determination to pursue that area. It is certainly worth the time and effort to find out what area a person seems to have the most natural ability for.

I started and oversaw a program at Shell where we brought in high school students through an organized province-wide program. The students worked as maintenance trade apprentices for a school semester. This gave the students a head start in becoming journeymen in their chosen trades. In the early days of this program, we encountered a number of well-intentioned teachers who pushed certain kids into the trades because they felt they were good, deserving kids but not smart enough to go to university. We spent a lot of time convincing teachers and program administrators that the trades made great careers for anyone who liked working with their hands irrespective of what their IQ might be. The theory applies really well in this case; if a person's abilities combine to make them especially good for millwright work, then that career is one in which they will have a high degree of success and gain a great deal of satisfaction. If such a person is also strong academically and they get pushed into university to eventually land a good-paying desk job, their work life will be far less fulfilling. The chances for promotions and greater responsibility in their field would be much better if they were a successful millwright instead of an unfulfilled desk worker. The high-performing millwright is likely to move into even higher-paying supervisor and management positions, or perhaps open and run his own business.

Chapter 3, on motivation, provides plenty of information on the keys to increasing learner motivation, while the chapter on ethics shows what behavior can decrease a learner's motivation. These are keys for enabling the greatest degree of determination and hard work in the student. Learning anything, especially in the beginning, is challenging and difficult for anyone, period. Good teaching gets students through this stage and on to where they can see what their abilities are in the area of study.

CHAPTER 5

Needs Analysis

INTRODUCTION

IN ACADEMIC SETTINGS, needs analyses are typically complex and very detailed. Depending on the subject, the audience, and the situation, needs analyses can be as detailed in industry or corporate settings. They can also be simple and straightforward. Using a competency profile as the need analysis approach can be simple to complex depending on the scope and detail required. This flexibility is what has made the needs analysis quite popular. For this chapter I've chosen to focus on and describe the process of developing and using competency profiles. These are an effective approach to developing a needs analysis.

COMPETENCY PROFILES

THE TERM *COMPETENCY* is commonly misunderstood. A competency is a combination of three elements: knowledge, skill, and attitude. A competency is not just one of these three elements. A collection of related competencies can be organized into a competency profile. A competency, strictly defined, is the smallest combination of knowledge and skill(s) that is required to execute a task. For example, skid control when driving a car is one competency of the many needed to drive a car. That said, it can be more practical and workable to look at competencies as bigger elements. For example, driving a car is one big competency with a number of elements.

If we consider driving a car, a competent driver would need to have knowledge of the rules of the road (e.g., what traffic light colors mean, what different signs mean, what side of the road to drive on). In addition to this knowledge, the driver needs to know how the car's controls work, what each of the pedals does, what the steering wheel does, where the switches are to turn on the lights, when the driver should turn on the lights, and so on. Beyond this, to be fully competent, a driver should know what he can do to better avoid accidents, how to control a skid, and how the car dynamically functions (e.g., when the brakes are applied, the car shifts its weight forward, allowing greater traction by the front tires and removing traction for the rear tires), along with the implications each function. The driver then needs the skills to know how much to turn the steering wheel to make a given turn, the skill to turn the steering wheel the right amount to control a skid while at the same time easing up the precise amount on the gas pedal, the skill to operate the gas pedal and the clutch pedal in a manual transmission while using his hand to shift gears, and so on.

To teach a person how to drive, all the required knowledge and skills could be listed out and organized into groups that are related. This would provide a competency profile of what knowledge and skills a driver would need to gain to be a competent driver. Before we go any farther, did I mention that competency includes attitude? In the case of competency, we are not talking about a good or positive attitude, or a negative or bad attitude. In this case, the reference is to where a person's attitude is on a scale ranging from timid to aggressive. For example, suppose someone has all the knowledge involved in driving a car and also has exceptional skill for every aspect of driving, but when she arrives at a stop sign, she is so afraid, so timid, that she will not proceed unless the closest approaching car is over half a mile (one kilometer) away. Even though she has all the knowledge and skill for the competency of driving, she would rate very low on the competency scale of driving as a result of her attitude. The same would be true of a driver who is too aggressive. For driving, the high-competence attitude is one of being conservatively assertive.

Many industries are moving to competency-based systems for their learning and development. By determining what competencies are required for a given job role, the knowledge and skills required to successfully accomplish the job can be determined. Once the knowledge and skills are known, a person in the job can be assessed to determine if he has the required knowledge and skills and to what degree. The appropriate learning can then be assigned.

A competency profile lists all the tasks required to successfully execute a job and organizes these tasks in such a way that the related tasks are grouped together. The following description illustrates a section of a competency profile for a learning department's administrative assistant:

1.0 Arrange training courses.
    1.1 Check availability of rooms.

      1.2 Book rooms.

      1.3 Arrange catering.

      1.4 Enter course date into the LMS.

      1.5 Assign students.

      1.6 Set up the room.

      1.7 Print and distribute name cards.

2.0 Manage the LMS.

      2.1 Create courses in the LMS.

      2.2 Run compliance reports.

      2.3 Build curriculums.

      2.4 Assign courses.

      2.5 Assign curriculums.

      2.6 Assign retraining frequency to courses.

3.0 Maintain learning inventory.

      3.1 Perform learning resource inventory check.

      3.2 Order new course materials.

      3.3 Organize inventory.

      3.4 Monitor resource sign-out.

      3.5 Deliver learning resources for courses.

4.0 Keep records.

      4.1 ...

A competency profile needs to include all the tasks for a given job. This is easier said than done. A reasonably thorough competency profile will have at least 100 competencies listed. Typically, 130 to 180 competencies provide the detail necessary for building learning and curriculums. I have found the best approach is to hold a group session with people who are currently doing the job. The first step is to define to the team what the terms *competency, knowledge, skill,* and *task* mean. Next, have them individually write all the tasks of their job on sticky notes, and have them place these sticky notes on a wall. Once this step is completed, ask the group to organize the tasks into related groupings. Once this has been completed, review each grouping with the team, remove duplicates, discuss what was missed and needs to be added, and agree on the best phrasing. This process can take over a day. From experience I've found that holding two separate sessions works well. In the first session, the initial brainstorming takes place as does a general organizing of the tasks. The following day or week (don't wait more than a week), the second session takes place; typically the people come with more tasks they thought of, and the brainstorming continues.

In many cases this is not a practical approach, such as when a new manufacturing plant is being built and no front-line workers have been hired. In a case where the actual people doing the job are not available, other people in the organization who are knowledgeable of what the job entails need to be enlisted to perform the process outlined above.

Once you have a competency profile, each task needs to be analyzed for what knowledge and skills are required to execute it. All the knowledge and skills will be listed, and there will likely be duplicates that can be stroked off. Then each required knowledge and skill item needs to be examined to determine how an individual would gain that particular knowledge or skill. It could be on the job from a mentor, from a formal training course, and/or part of a development plan.

I did this for an oil sand upgrader being built, and for part of it we had all the equipment listed, what type of maintenance trade would be required, and what types of repairs would need to be performed on the equipment. This enabled the company to know what trades to hire, how many to hire, and what experience to look for in the applicants. The competency profile guided our training, and we assigned each task several criteria for each applicant to be judged on. We examined the following:

- The criticality of the equipment. If it were to fail, would it result in a very expensive plant shutdown, or would an online spare simply come online?
- How complex the equipment was. Was it something an experienced journeyman could likely repair with nothing more than a manual, or was the equipment very complex, indicating specialized training would be required?
- How readily available outside support was. In some cases the vendor was only minutes away, while in other cases the vendor was on the other side of the Atlantic Ocean.
- Whether regulatory training was required. For example, some instrumentation uses a low-energy radioactive source, and small as it may be, it is still government regulated, so anyone working on it needs training approved by the government.
- How confident we felt, that we could hire people experienced in repairing this equipment. The duration of the training plan was for a three-year period, so if we could hire people with a great deal of experience, then training would be a lower priority and could be pushed off until the third year.

We assessed these criteria for each piece of equipment and then determined the training required and how many people would need to be trained. A three-year plan and schedule was developed that guided us in contacting and scheduling training suppliers. The three-year plan allowed us to create a detailed budget.

In some cases, a job entails more than just the technical side of executing the work. In the chemical, oil and gas, and manufacturing workplace, and in many other workplaces, safety is a large component that must be assessed. At Dow Chemical, each task on a competency profile was further assessed for what safety, knowledge, and skills were required to execute or oversee/supervise each task. This ensured each employee had all the safety competencies they needed to be safe in executing their jobs. The same exercise was applied to determine soft skills and leadership competencies needed to perform the job role and the training required to fill those gaps. I am sure there are other industries where a competency profile is used for other perspectives in determining the learning and development needed for particular jobs.

Let us take this one step further. In order to execute a task, the knowledge and skill(s) required needs to be specific in order to determine if existing training will provide what is required or in order to develop training for the task(s). For example, I had plant operations come to me and say we needed to train our field operators on how to safely perform basic maintenance. They had had some incidents and close calls. I met with the field operators and asked what maintenance activities they performed on shift and also what maintenance activities they felt they should be performing. Next, I took that list to a meeting with their supervisors and management and asked if this was what we wanted operators to do for on-shift maintenance tasks. Once the maintenance tasks were agreed to, I created a needs analysis that drove the development of the training.

The group determined that the operators needed to be able to perform a variety of minor maintenance jobs. These jobs were grouped under the following basic headings:

1. Perform basic pipe fitting on piping up to two inches in diameter: connecting flanges, torqueing, threading pipe, connecting threaded pipe.
2. Work with tubing up to three-quarters of an inch in diameter: bend, connect, dissemble, replace fittings, and

connect to piping (know/recognize the difference between pipe and tubing threads).

3. Assemble and disassemble piping connection hubs including blind hubs.
4. Install and remove piping blind flanges up to six inches in diameter.
5. Be able to draw and read isometric drawings for the purpose of assembling piping according to a design.

Each of these categories was broken down for the knowledge and skills required and then cross-checked with the original list of jobs to ensure teaching this knowledge and these skills would enable the operators to successfully execute the work. This produced the following list:

1a. Screw pipe together.
1b. Run sections of piping.
1c. Install fitting plug.
1d. Correct use of piping tape and piping compound.
1e. Remove blind end from a hub.
1f. Install a two-inch flanged valve.
1g. Select correct spec pipe fittings for a given job.
1h. Select correct gaskets for a job.
1i. Select and use proper tools.
1j. Select and properly apply thread lubricants or lockers.
1k. Use rigging to support piping.
1l. Select and use the correct fasteners.
1m. Measure, cut, and thread a specified length of pipe.
1n. Install a union.
1o. Connect hose fittings to piping.
1p. Perform a hydro leak test.
2a. Bend tubing to a prescribed angle.
2b. Tighten a tubing fitting (know the procedure).

2c. Cut tubing.

2d. Be able to distinguish piping thread from piping threads.

Etc.

I won't list all the knowledge and skills for all the remaining categories, but as you've noticed, each list gets progressively more detailed and subsequently longer. Training was designed from this list of knowledge and skills (see Chapter 18: Competency Assurance). The instructional design included classroom instruction with demonstrations and some small hands-on activities, supplemented with videos.

The classroom instruction was supplemented with a pipe fitting handbook given to each student. The handbook covered more than what we would instruct on, but it was a great reference source for the students. For the instruction that was covered in the handbook, we referenced the corresponding pages in the handbook. For example, the following is part of the list, as the full list is the longest of them all. I present this to give you an idea of what the steps from needs analysis through to the instructional design plan look like:

- Explanation of company's internal pipe specs and where to find them
- Piping schedules, reference diagram from p. 15
- Pipe sizes go by ID up to twelve-inch pipe, them by OD, whereas tubing only goes by OD
- Piping chart(s), pp. 19–42
- Pipe ends, p. 43 diagrams
- Different types of pipe, pp. 45–80
- Different valves, pp. 117–22, valve diagrams
- Screwed valve connection tightening, diagram, p. 149
- Elbows, p. 162
- Unions, p. 165
- Couplings, p. 166

- Tees, wyes, and crosses, p. 167
- Fittings classes, p. 178
- Etc.

To ensure the students were competent and that they learned what was instructed, they were taken to the maintenance shop, where they were given an isometric drawing and a crate of piping and tubing fittings. The students were required to assemble the parts according to the drawing. There were extra fittings in the crates, and some fittings were intentionally faulty; the students needed to determine this during assembly. Finally, they had to perform a hydrostatic leak test on their piping assembly to ensure it was leak-free.

CONCLUSION

NEEDS ANALYSIS IS the foundation of any learning program. There are several methods that can be used to determine the learning needs. Whatever method is chosen, it is vital that all the knowledge and skills required are determined. The instructional design and curriculum development are based on the needs analysis. The more detailed and precise the needs analysis, the better the instructional design will be in meeting the learner's needs.

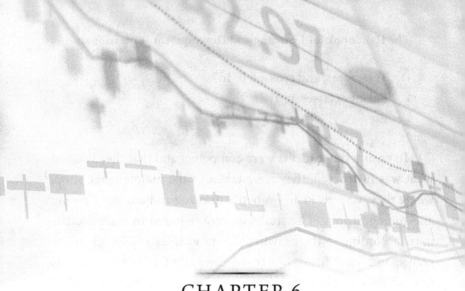

CHAPTER 6

Curriculum Development

INTRODUCTION

CURRICULUMS IN THE workplace are typically quite different from those developed in the K–12 system. K–12 curriculums focus on a set number of weeks (a school semester) and what needs to be covered each week. In K–12 schools, the teacher owns the curriculum and provides all the learning direction. A workplace-based curriculum, on the other hand, is the combination of learning elements required to perform a job. The elements are clearly defined with regard to learning outcomes but may consist of formal classroom training, online training, self-study, peer-to-peer on-the-job learning, and coaching by a trainer or mentor. The worker typically owns his curriculum and progresses through it at his pace, a pace that is likely negotiated and agreed to with his supervisor/manager.

Note that a complete job may have more than one curriculum. For example, a worker in a chemical plant may have three curriculums, one for environmental and safety, one for soft skills training, and one for the technical aspects of her particular job. There is no precise formula for developing a curriculum, other than it should be a logical combination of learning elements designed to accomplish a stated goal. In the case of the example given, the goal would be to provide the worker with all the knowledge and skills required to perform a particular job in the chemical plant. All the workers performing that role would be assigned the same three curriculums.

Within the curriculums there can also be optionality. For example, for a team of six shippers/receivers, the technical curriculum might include operating a forklift as an optional course decided by the supervisors as a result of only half the team needing forklift training. Similarly, for the soft skills curriculum, the employees may have to take three core courses and then have their choice of taking three out of another five courses that are offered within the curriculum.

IMPORTANCE OF TAXONOMIES

FROM YOUR NEEDS analysis, you know what the curriculum needs to contain. For example, it may have been determined that the shippers/receivers in the previous example are required to know about their company's shipping logistics, which involves both rail and truck shipments of the products. The question then becomes how much and to what degree do they need to understand the company's logistics business. Bloom's taxonomy is good way of analyzing a topic to be learned and assessing to what degree or level it needs to be learned. This knowledge can then be used in the curriculum, which in turn drives the proper instructional design. Learning taxonomies allows for determining the degree or level to which a particular learning objective is learned and can be evaluated in terms of its depth or how complex it is to master.

Benjamin Bloom came up with the idea of creating a classification of statements around what students were intended to learn from instruction. The idea was for various universities to be able to share and create banks of test items for testing educational objectives. Bloom gathered a group of measurement specialists who met twice a year starting in 1949. In 1956, the group published *Taxonomy of Educational Objectives: The Classification of Educational Goals. Handbook 1: Cognitive Domain* (Bloom et al. 1956). This taxonomy (see appendix A) has six levels: knowledge, comprehension, application, analysis, synthesis, and evaluation. These are broken down into subsections, except for the application level. The levels progress from simple to more and more complex. The taxonomy is a cumulative hierarchy where mastery of the first level is required in order to move up to the next level, and so on.

Krathwohl (2002) revised the Bloom et al. (1956) taxonomy (see appendix B). Where the original taxonomy focused mostly on developing the six main categories that make up the foundation, the revised version resulted in some changes to this foundation. Most of the focus and, hence, changes were to the subcategories, which then more clearly described the main categories. The revised version is not as strict as the original as it allows some overlapping, but it is still very much a hierarchy. The revised version added a section for metacognitive levels.

The Quellmalz framework (see appendix C), a modified version of the Bloom et al. (1956) original taxonomy, is a framework consisting of an educational objective taxonomy with only five levels: recall, analysis, comparison, inference, and evaluation. Gronlund (1998) observed that many teachers find the Quellmalz framework taxonomy easier to use. The category descriptions are stated in more of a verb and noun style than the original taxonomy (Quellmalz 1987). I have a preference for the Quellmalz framework as I've found that in the workplace the five-level Quellmalz framework provides sufficient detail and works well. My preference aside, each of these taxonomies allows for determining the degree to which a particular learning objective needs to be learned. A learning objective can be evaluated in terms of its depth or how complex it is to master. Conversely, a learned topic can be tested against the criteria to determine to what degree or according to what complexity level the topic was learned.

Going back to our shippers/receivers example, it would likely be determined they would require learning up to the second or third level in any of the discussed taxonomies, whereas people working in the company's logistics department, depending on their job, would require learning from level three up to the highest or second-highest level. Applying the taxonomy to the needs analysis negates the possibility of providing the same training to everyone in the logistics department as well as to all the shippers/receivers. Often, an all-encompassing course is developed and everyone whose job involves any aspect of that topic gets a whole training course or courses, even if they only require a portion of what is covered. By applying an educational objectives taxonomy, courses appropriate for different levels of learners can be identified. This of course eliminates a lot of time unnecessarily spent in training. Furthermore, having employees sit through training that is of very little value to them reduces their confidence in the L & D team and sullies their attitude on future training, which might be 100 percent relevant.

The following are three curriculum examples built for shippers/receivers, one curriculum for their environmental, health, and safety (EHS) training, a second one for their technical training requirements, and the third one for their interpersonal (soft skills) training.

Group: Shippers/Receivers

1. EHS curriculum name: LMS code name—CDN_AB_S/R_Environment_Health_Safety

Curriculum purpose/goal: To provide employees with all the environmental, health, and safety training required to enable them to safely perform their job roles. Accomplish this through the use of appropriate training resources and delivery methods providing the employee with the greatest amount of flexibility.

Standards/policies/practices: Company's relevant documents, EHS practices, needs analysis, requirements, etc.

Summary: The following courses need to be taken with refresher training before expiration dates. The courses are independent of one another and can be taken in any order. All courses can be registered for through the LMS. All courses are offered on-site.

Courses:

- Transportation of Dangerous Goods, two-hour online course
  - Covers definitions, classifications, shipping documentation, containers, ERP plans, reporting, and markings. This course requires retraining/certification every three years. Requires passing an online exam.

- WHMIS 2015, two-hour online course.
  - Covers definitions, hazards, appropriate personal protective equipment (PPE), safety information, symbols/labels, safety data sheets (MSDS), and rights and responsibilities. Requires passing an online exam.
- Fire Extinguisher Use, four-hour classroom/field course.
  - Covers care and operation, types of fires (classes), techniques, and practical use in extinguishing live fires. Required to pass written and practical test.
- First Aid/CPR, two-day (sixteen-hour) classroom/ practical course
  - Covers level C CPR and choking for adults, shock and unconsciousness, head and spinal injuries, severe bleeding, major medical conditions, AED, and fractures of the upper and lower limbs. Required to pass written and practical test.
- Scene Securement, one-hour online course
  - Covers whom to notify, how to secure the scene of an incident, and what immediate steps need to be taken. No assessment required.
- Spill Response, three-hour classroom course
  - Covers notifications, care and use of spill kits, preventive measures, and primary and secondary containment. Requires passing an online exam.
- Proper Lifting Technique, thirty-minute online and one-and-a-half-hour classroom/practical course.
  - Covers lifting allowed amounts, proper lifting technique (theory and practice), and how to prepare. Requires passing an online test.

2. Technical curriculum name: LMS code name—CDN_
   AB_S/R_Warehouse_Specifics

Curriculum purpose/goal: Provide employees with all the knowledge and skills they need to perform all the required duties of a shipper/receiver. Accomplish this through the use of appropriate training resources and delivery methods, providing the employee with the greatest amount of flexibility.

Standards/policies/practices: Warehouse procedures and practices.

Summary: The following courses need to be taken with refresher training before expiration dates. The courses are independent of one another and can be taken in any order. All courses can be registered for through the LMS. All courses are offered on-site.

Courses:

Review of Warehouse Procedures, individual twenty-minute online courses
   – Covers shipping process and procedures, receiving process and procedures, TDG and WHMIS document storage and application, and safety plans. Each module requires passing an online exam.
Forklift, eight-hour classroom/field course
   – Covers government regulations, company forklift practice, peruse inspection safety checks, safe maneuvering, refueling, stability triangle, inclines and declines, lifting, transporting, and lowering. Requires passing a written and practical field test.

XYZ Warehouse Computer System, two-hour classroom, two-hour self-study
- – Covers electronic inventory system, shipping and receiving tracking, online TDG and WHMIS documentation, and purchasing. No assessment is required.

Trailer Backing, four-hour classroom/field course
- – Covers visibility, spotter, signals, techniques, dangers, and practical application and practice. Requires passing both a written and field test.

3. Interpersonal skills curriculum name: LMS code name—CDN_AB_S/R_Soft_Skills

Curriculum purpose/goal: Provide employees with the necessary interpersonal knowledge and skills to be effective shippers/receivers in a collaborative team working environment. Accomplish this through the use of appropriate training resources and delivery methods, providing the employee with the greatest amount of flexibility.

Standards/policies/practices: HR policies.

Summary: The core courses need to be taken first and in numerical order. The other courses can be taken in any order; an employee can only take one optional course per year unless he or she has a supervisor's approval.

Courses:
Core 1—Effective Communication, four-hour classroom course
- – Covers emotional awareness, communication styles, keywords, and active listening. No assessment is required.

Core 2—Conflict Resolution, four-hour classroom course
- Covers roots of conflict, escalation, misunderstandings, common ground, skills for resolving, strategies for calming, and skill development. No assessment is required.

Core 3—Collaborative Teamwork, four-hour classroom course
- Covers shared goals, relationships, coaching, collaboration, stages, feedback, and skill development. No assessment is required.

Option 1: The 7 Habits, eight-hour classroom course
- FranklinCovey *7 Habits of Highly Effective People* course; includes a copy of the text. No assessment is required.

Option 2: Level 1 Leadership, eight-hour classroom course
- Covers coaching techniques, how to communicate change, advanced listening skills, problem analysis, delegating, and decision-making. No assessment is required.

Option 3: Project Leader, four-hour classroom course
- Covers identifying communication barriers, developing project timelines, milestones, effective meetings, and project software. No assessment is required.

CONCLUSION

WORKPLACE CURRICULUMS VARY significantly from K–12 curriculums. Workplace curriculums aim to assemble related learning for a particular job into one collection. Using an educational taxonomy such as Bloom's or Quellmalz's will aid in identifying the level of knowledge required to be addressed in the curriculum for each training course. Finally, it is good practice to outline the details of the courses held within each curriculum as shown in the previous example.

CHAPTER 7

Instructional Design

INTRODUCTION

IN THE INTRODUCTION to *The Handbook for Learning and Development Professionals*, I noted that to fully cover most chapters in this book, an entire book or books could be written on the topic addressed in each chapter. This chapter is a good example of that. In the first part of this chapter I will cover a lot of the theoretical ground that underlines instructional design. This will provide a general overview of the foundations underpinning good instructional design. Beyond the theoretical basis for instructional design, the ADDIE model of instruction design and ISD principles will be outlined. A reference for the theoretical aspects covered in this chapter is found in a very good book on the subject written by Reigeluth and Carr-Chellman (2009). If you wish to dig deeper into the subject than I do in this chapter, I highly recommend their book *Instructional-Design Theories and Models, Volume III: Building a Common Knowledge Base.*

The idea of instructional design is to create a plan for how the learner will gain the knowledge and/or skills identified from the needs analysis. For this, the designer needs to know the learners, as well as what background prepares them for this learning. For example, let's say a company is acquiring new learning management system (LMS) software and you need to design instructional content for teaching the LMS administrators how to use the software. The instructional design will be different if the students are experienced with using other brands of LMS software, versus having never used or even seen LMS software before. The same material will have to be taught, but how? And what will the exercises be? This will all vary depending on the students. How large or small will the group be? The instructional design will be different if the instructor has a class size of six students versus having a class of sixty students. The designer needs to determine what content is most appropriate for instruction (i.e., that which is done *to* the learners) and what would be better suited to a construction design (i.e., that which is done *by* the learners). A great number of factors need to be considered before beginning the design process. Time spent planning will be greatly rewarded later during implementation.

PRACTICAL TIP

A LOT OF online training comes with screenshots or PowerPoint-type slides through which the learner advances. In many cases the text is narrated and the learner cannot advance until the narration is completed. This is bad form and inhibits learning. Yet I see it all the time. The learner needs to be able to turn off the narration and progress at his own pace. What happens is that the learner sees the text and starts to read it at his own internal pace, which in most cases will be far faster than the narration. If the reading pace is different from the listening pace, the brain gets frustrated about having to deal with two sources of input, and this inhibits the comprehension of what is being conveyed. The best approach for this type of learning is to have relevant diagrams, pictures, or media displayed while a voice teaches the learner, versus simply reading the displayed text.

INSTRUCTIONAL THEORY

DESIGN THEORY IS defined as being goal-oriented and normative. It attempts to identify the best methods for accomplishing goals. Design theory is the foundation of instructional design theory (IDT). Instructional theory is made up of six major types of IDT: instructional event theory, instructional analysis theory, instructional planning theory, instructional building theory, instructional implementation theory, and instructional evaluation theory.

Student assessment design theory integrates student assessment with instruction. The assessment feedback channels back into each of the six IDTs and enable the students to adjust and maximize the instructional results. For example, say the students fare poorly learning a particular segment. The instructional design will allow for review or returning to the concepts in future lessons. The feedback will also affect changes to the design of that section in future courses.

Curriculum design theory is concerned with what should be learned. Whereas student assessment design theory provides input at the application stage, curriculum design theory is applied in the design phase (i.e., the nuts and bolts of sequencing, timing, type of delivery, exercise type, and so on).

Instructional science focuses on developing knowledge about both learning (descriptive theory) and instructional events (design theory). Instructional design is really the meshing of these two theories.

Typically, there are seven layers within the design:

1. *Content layer* focuses on the various ways the content can be structured. Examples include sets of rules, sets of tasks, and sets of propositions.
2. *Strategy layer* is the layer in which the designer specifies the organization and properties of learning events, including student roles, responsibilities, goals, and timelines.
3. *Message layer* addresses ways that individual messages are employed to communicate content and other related information to the student. An example is how learner feedback is received, incorporated, and relayed.
4. *Control layer* includes options the learners have for taking action, in essence, how the student is able to carry out her side of the instructional conversation, for example, by asking questions and contributing responses.
5. *Representation layer* deals with methods by which messages will be delivered to the learner's senses, including the media that will be used and how different sources will be synchronized.
6. *Media logic layer* dictates how the various media will be employed to carry out the instructional events.
7. *Data management layer* is the learning management system layer. This layer determines what data is retained in the system for archiving, analysis, interpretation, and reporting.

A quality instructional design will have interaction between these seven layers and the six types of instructional theory.

An instructional design example most us are familiar with is the industrial age model; this is likely the design you were exposed to as a K–12 student. With this design, all students learn the same thing at the same time and pace. What typically happens with this model is that the slow learners (for a particular topic) get left behind, while the fast learners for that topic get bored and lose motivation. With the aid of technology, we're seeing a shift toward a student-centered model. It's tough to change, though, because of the great paradox. Most parents, while not having great things to say about their personal K–12 school experiences, insist that anything new in the school system is not as good as the old ways by which they were taught and thereby resist changes for their children.

INSTRUCTIONAL METHODS

DETERMINING THE INSTRUCTIONAL method for each topic within the overall program of instruction is both an art and a science. It starts with examining your needs analysis. What is it precisely that needs to be learned, who will be the students, what resources do you have available, what are the time constraints, and so on? The art part of this is the ability to determine what a good learning method is versus what is not a good approach for teaching a particular student group a specific topic. Most of us can likely think of many examples where the content was technically correct and organized, but the lesson plan really just fell flat on its face.

In Chapter 6: Needs Analysis, I discussed the operator basic maintenance training for which my company performed a needs analysis. In examining the breakdown of what needed to be learned, why it needed to be learned, by whom it would be learned, and how it would be used, we arrived at what we felt were the best approaches. For example, in performing small maintenance tasks, the operators might have to perform some very simple, straightforward rigging. What was important was that they recognize when it was required and what it should look like. This is mostly a knowledge component, so the instructional design we came up with was classroom based. Approximately 70 percent was lecture supported by media for examples, and 30 percent was demonstration coupled with in-classroom practice for some of the basics. Conversely, for the pipe fitting tasks that were identified in the needs analysis, these were tasks the operators would perform fairly often in the field; fitting a temporary section of piping together that does not leak is vital. For this part of the instructional design, we went with a short (ninety-minute) lecture covering the basic elements and all the safety aspects. This was followed by an afternoon in the shop where the students assembled a section of piping from a schematic drawing while being overseen and coached by journeymen pipe fitters. It is all a matter of examining what the topic is, knowing how the learner will apply it, determining who the learner is, and knowing the learner's background. Knowing these details will help guide you in coming up with the right method of instruction for that particular topic.

BASIC PRINCIPLES OF INSTRUCTIONAL DESIGN

KNOWLEDGE AND SKILLS that can be applied in more than one specific situation are referred to as generalizable knowledge and/or skills. These types of knowledge and skills are typically defined as how-to, type, and what happens. A simple example of this is the knowledge that turning a bolt clockwise will tighten it and turning it counterclockwise will loosen it. In any circumstance where turning a bolt is required, the same how-to knowledge and skill will apply. Ordinarily the generalizable knowledge and/or skill will be more complex than this, but it will show up repeatedly in your needs analysis. The instructional design will have determined the best place to teach the topic and obviously to recognize when it has been taught earlier in a course—and therefore when it applies in the later part of the lesson, it will not need to be retaught. The topic may require review, and what that looks like will be incorporated in the instructional design.

TASK-CENTERED PRINCIPLE

LEARNING IS IMPROVED when students engage in task-centered instruction. This instructional strategy involves using progressions, that is, moving from simple tasks to more and more complex tasks. If you took drafting in high school, you remember you had to draft a number of drawings throughout the semester. In these drawings, on one page you had to show the side, top, and end views. The course started with having to draw a simple shape, and typically the end and top views were simply different-size rectangles that aligned with the side view. As the course progressed through the semester, the drawings became increasingly more complex and difficult.

ACTIVATION PRINCIPLE

LEARNING IS ENHANCED when students apply previous knowledge and/or skills in learning a new topic. In chapter 3, we discussed Knowles, Holton, and Swanson's (2015) adult learning theory or, as it is sometimes referred to, andragogy theory, so we know that applying previous knowledge and experiences in learning is especially helpful for adults. The instructional design needs to stimulate learners to recall previous related experiences and connect these to the new learning. Peer discussions and sharing of experiences is helpful. As an example, if you do not know how to tie a reef knot and if you have someone teach you how (or you search the Web for a video), you immediately relate the first step of the reef knot to the first step in tying your shoes. There are basically two steps to tying a reef knot, and without really learning anything new, you already know half of what you need to learn. Tapping into learners' experiences and relating them to the new material being taught is a very effective approach to use in instructional design.

DEMONSTRATION PRINCIPLE

A DEMONSTRATION CAN help students to better understand and learn. Demonstrations are great for starting discussion, which further promotes learning. Most demonstrations should encourage discussion along with questioning. The demonstration needs be narrated to aid the overall instruction. Demonstrations do not necessarily need to be face-to-face; they can be done from a distance. The media chosen needs to be appropriate for the demonstration. The instructional design determines the complexity of the topic for the learners. At a certain level of complexity, the demonstration will require progressions leading up to the final demonstration. Even something as simple as swinging a golf club is complex to a point, so to be taught effectively, it requires demonstration and practice in progressions. This is true even for someone who has played golf for a long time but has a flaw in her swing.

APPLICATION PRINCIPLE

AS THE NAME suggests, learning is improved when students are given an opportunity to practice the knowledge and/or skills they have just learned. The setting for the practice should be organized so the instructor or another skilled person is immediately available for coaching and guiding the application as it was taught. As the application of the knowledge and/or skill progresses, less coaching will be required, and it is important for the instructor to realize he should step aside and allow the students to work their way through the exercise and have their own aha moments. If possible, peer discussion and collaboration should be factored into the instructional design. When applying the knowledge in a realistic simulated exercise, peer-to-peer learning can be very powerful.

INTEGRATION PRINCIPLE

IF LEARNERS DO not apply newly learned knowledge or skills, they'll forget fairly quickly. But if the learners apply the newfound knowledge and skills, this not only helps them to retain the knowledge but also can help further their understanding. Instructional design should help learners identify where in their lives or work they can apply the new knowledge and/or skills. Follow-up peer discussion can augment the learning and retention. This discussion could take place online with the instructor assigning a couple of questions that all the students are required to respond to in order to get the discussion and sharing started.

COMBINING PRINCIPLES INTO THE INSTRUCTIONAL DESIGN

THE FIVE PRINCIPLES (demonstration, application, task[s], activation, and integration) should all be combined in an instructional design. They do not all have to be used, and sometimes it is not practical to do so. However, the more principles that are combined, the greater the eventual quality of the instruction. For each subtopic, the design would go from task, to activation of the student, to demonstrating, to application, to integration of learning. Then repeat the cycle for the next subtopic. One would expect the instructional approaches to vary from subtopic to subtopic. At the same time, certain processes are occurring that support the five principles. Structure, guidance, coaching, and reflection are being performed by the instructor to support the learners as they progress through the instructional design for each subtopic.

If you're going to incorporate problem-based learning into your instructional design, strive to make it a real-world problem. It is far more effective to have a task that exists in the real world versus an imaginary problem. The temptation is to think that a make-believe problem can be better designed and controlled, not to mention likely being a lot less work for the instructor. While a real-world problem might not be the ideal fit and can provide surprises, using a real problem is much more effective and far outweighs any drawbacks.

SITUATIONAL ASPECTS OF INSTRUCTION

SITUATIONAL PRINCIPLES DEAL with items that are not universal but that only apply in certain specific situations. At some point in the course of learning, some practice or a learner activity of some kind may be called for, and these types of exercises are universally good for all instruction. However, the exact type of practice is situational, so it will be different for math instruction than for learning communication skills, or for learning to swing a golf club, and so on. Instruction tends to be a heuristic task. One cannot lay out a step-by-step communication script for teaching. There will be questions, but an instructor cannot know what all the questions will be in advance, and even if she could, she would not be able to know what the reaction to the explanations will be. In addition to this, the student(s) may be overly excited or depressed, so the students' moods need to be responded to appropriately by the instructor. It is simply not possible to have a precise script for teaching. For example, you can learn the principles to greeting and meeting someone, but there is no exact script you can follow.

Examples of situational factors (situationalities) based on different instructional approaches include direct instruction, discussion, peer learning, experiential learning, problem-based learning, and simulation-based learning. Examples of situationalities based on different learning outcomes include knowledge, comprehension, application, analysis, evaluation, and affective development.

THEORY OF THE DIRECT APPROACH TO INSTRUCTION

A. Presentation phase
   1. **Review.** Instructor and students review previously learned material that is relevant to or a prerequisite of the new learning material.
   2. **What.** Instructor describes and outlines the new knowledge and skills to be learned. Students are informed as explicitly as possible of what they should be able to perform at the end of the learning process and how the student is to be held accountable.
   3. **Why.** Instructor explains the material to be learned and why it is important.
   4. **Explanation.** Instructor discusses the relationship of new learning material to other topics and their components.

Typically this is accomplished with the strong use of examples.

5. **Probing and responding.** Instructor provides ample opportunities for the students to demonstrate their initial understanding of the learning material. This is both a summative and a formative evaluation. The instructor uses this formative feedback to make adjustments to the learning plan.

B. Practice phase
1. **Guided practice.** Practice is executed with admonition, and supervision is provided by the instructor.
2. **Independent practice.** Students practice on their own.
3. **Periodic review.** Instructor periodically goes back and reviews previous material and, where possible, explains its connection to newer learning.

C. Assessment and evaluation phase
1. **Formative assessment.** Instructor makes formative valuation decisions on student progress on a daily basis and makes corresponding adjustments.
2. **Summative evaluation.** Instructor gathers summative data though some form of formal testing to determine student success. This is typically executed on a weekly basis or at the end of a shorter course.

D. Monitoring and feedback
1. **Cues and prompts.** Instructor uses cues and prompts along with questioning and probing in reviewing previous material with students.
2. **Corrective feedback.** As the instructor performs student assessments during a lesson, he or she provides both corrective and reinforcing feedback.

Direct instruction has been shown to be very effective. The influence of operant conditioning and behavior analysis is fairly obvious in the direct instruction approach. This approach clearly advocates stating explicit observable objectives and breaking down learning into small steps with correction and reinforcement of mastery of each step. Essentially it is teaching what the final test will contain or teaching to the test. If the course material or design is intended to develop higher-level or critical thinking, then direct instruction is a poor choice. The critics of standardized testing in K–12 schools take opposition to this approach as it narrows the curriculum, pushing teachers to teach to the test only. They feel, and rightly so I believe, that this limits the learning and development of the students. While I agree, I think standardized testing is good for certain subjects, such as math and a great deal of the material for kindergarten and grades 4–6, where a solid base needs to be built. But by the time students are attending high school, the curriculum should be more focused on developing critical-thinking ability.

High school students taking science and learning about contemporary topics should be broadening their thinking and being critical in their thinking. For example, high school science students should be free to challenge climate change, as long as they can make solid arguments supported by reputable references, versus being taught strictly what the answer is. At the high school level, students should be researching, thinking critically, and discovering. All theories are just that: theories, not facts. Even theories that become laws, for example, Newton's universal law of gravitation, have been shown not to hold in places of our universe. In high school, students need to learn how to question, understand, and think critically. Learning at a higher level is achieved in part through others challenging one's positions and perceived knowledge. It becomes a pursuit of the truth. Truth, like perfection, is pursued with the knowledge that it will never be reached, but the journey brings growth. The point is that besides learning the core knowledge, time spent developing higher-level and critical thinking will be far more valuable in the future. The only use for a standardized test at this higher level would be simply to administer it as pass or fail. At this level, teaching to the test is a disservice to the students, although there is a core of knowledge they need to master if they expect to succeed in postsecondary education.

DISCUSSION APPROACH TO INSTRUCTION

COMMONLY KNOWN AS discussion teaching, this method has active learning at its core. By nature, it is inclusive and very much participatory. This approach is organized to do the following:

- create shared responsibility for teaching and learning,
- promote the sharing of students' experiences and worldviews,
- utilize democratic participation in the teaching and learning dynamic,
- develop critical-thinking and problem-solving skills, and
- develop a community of learners who work together in the pursuit of knowledge.

This approach is well suited for topics where in-depth exploration and the interaction of ideas from people of multiple perspectives will enhance learning (e.g., leadership training). This approach is not suited for topics where building specific knowledge-based areas is the primary focus, such as how to enter employees' time and exceptions into a payroll system.

This approach typically starts with the facilitator asking the group to respond to a question, asking students to summarize the main points of the prework, or placing the students in small groups with a complex question to respond to. The challenge then becomes how to keep the momentum of the discussion going. The idea is that lively discussions lead to new levels of understanding. The facilitator needs to have considered where the conversation may go and be ready with questions and resources to keep the conversation moving—and in the right direction.

This approach can be used in distance learning, but it does present some unique challenges in such a setting. For example, the instructor needs to consider how to foster interactions between students. Discussion boards can be used, but there will be a time lag between responses, which means that any spontaneity will be lost. The longer the time lag, the greater the problem, so the instructor needs to consider how to keep the discussion moving. Another concern is students' past experience with traditional learning settings where their participation memories might not be fond ones. These students will be hesitant to join in discussion. The instructor needs to be able to recognize this and have the ability to get them engaged and participating. This is often much easier said than done.

EXPERIENTIAL APPROACH TO INSTRUCTION

THIS APPROACH IN involves a real experience that has a cognitive challenge component. This type of learning is very much learner-centered with the students being actively involved. The students have a high degree of self-direction with this approach. As an example, I once took a class on kayaking. As part of this, we needed to learn how to perform a kayak roll, also referred to as an Eskimo roll, although I believe *Eskimo roll* is no longer considered politically correct terminology. But I digress. In order to successfully execute the maneuver, one needs to actually perform it (experience it), and once you do it, it's fairly easy to repeat, making you wonder why it took so many attempts to execute it the first time. Examples of experiential learning include learning a software program, running a particular meeting for the first time, or even tying one's shoes for the first time.

The first step in the experiential learning approach is to communicate the objectives and/or goals of the learning. Along with this, the criteria and method of assessment are communicated and negotiated with the students. The second step is to activate the experience. The experience needs to be as authentic as possible. The instructor keeps the focus on the problem and involves the learners in making decisions as they learn to overcome the problem. The last step is to reflect on the experience. The instructor facilitates deep reflection by challenging assumptions held by the students. The reflection is intended to help the students understand why and what happened, what was learned, and how to apply that learning.

PROBLEM-BASED APPROACH TO INSTRUCTION

THIS APPROACH IS rooted in experience-based learning. Learning through experience while solving a problem can develop both knowledge and thinking strategies. Problem-based, experiential, and indeed most instructional approaches are typically part of a combination of instructional design approaches interlocked for teaching a subject.

There are four basic steps to the problem-based approach:

1. Develop a meaningful real-world problem that contributes to learning the subject.

2. Have the instructor present the problem and get the students started in the right direction, possibly with some learning material. The instructor then becomes a guide, not a supplier of content. The students essentially create their own content.

3. Use authentic assessment practices in order.

   - Students assess their effectiveness as researchers and solvers of the problem or as contributors to the problem-solving process of a group.
   - Students reflect on knowledge gains and integration of that learning with their prior knowledge.
   - The proposed solution is assessed on criteria (e.g., accuracy, completeness, viability). These criteria can be developed by the students.

4. Have the instructor facilitate thorough debriefing activities to consolidate key concepts of the learning experience.

SIMULATION APPROACH TO INSTRUCTION

SIMULATIONS ARE A great way to gain knowledge and skills for a difficult task where real-world errors have serious consequences, such as learning to fly an airplane or learning to operate an oil and gas or chemical plant's computer control system. In these applications, simulations have proven to be very effective for learning and maintaining knowledge and skills.

Simulation involves one or more dynamic models that engage the learners in interactions that result in state changes. The process is aided by instructional components in the pursuit of one or more instructional objectives.

Microworld is a model-centered type of environment. Students construct a model using resources (e.g., parts, information, tools) supplied by the instructor. The learner proceeds on a self-directed path to explore and experiment in order to learn principles and relationships. The instructor is involved as a guide and coach.

Learning goals are employed to learn and gain understanding of principles and relationships in dynamic systems, and to develop skills and abilities for dealing with complex systems.

Fidelity, in relation to simulations, is the degree of resemblance between the simulation/model and reality. For example, suppliers like to use the term *high fidelity* for their simulators, which is okay as long as there are accepted criteria for applying a rating to the fidelity.

Task fidelity refers to how realistic the actions of the learner are. How closely do they mimic the actual environment they will be executed in?

Speed/timeliness refers to the resemblance of the simulation's/ model's time and response to the real-world time and response. In many simulations this can be sped up. For example, an operator starting up a process in a refinery in the real world may take twelve hours or more, so there's a lot of waiting. The waiting time can be eliminated in a simulation.

Accuracy refers to how accurately the simulation's or model's calculations or outputs mirror the real-world result.

ADDIE MODEL

THE ADDIE MODEL is a five-phase instructional systems design (ISD) approach to instructional design. The ADDIE acronym is derived from each of its five phases: analysis, design, development, implementation, and evaluation.

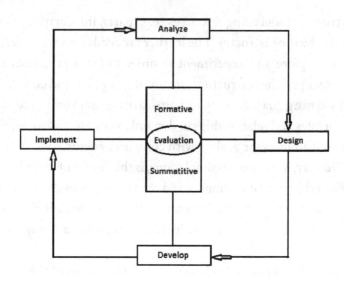

Analysis answers questions such as what the learning objectives are, who the learners will be, what the learning environment will be, what the content and delivery options are, and whether or not there are any time limitations. A thorough needs analysis aids this process.

Design ensures that learning objectives are matched with content, that delivery choices (e.g., lecture, experiences, media) are made, that prework (if required) is determined, that learning exercises are created, and that assessment criteria and methods are determined.

Development is the stage where the content is developed to match with the design delivery choices. Some form of evaluation takes place; it could be as simple as a thorough review or as complex as running a pilot and gathering feedback. At this point, adjustments are made to fill in any gaps or correct any disconnects.

Implementation begins as the instructors are briefed on the content, delivery approaches, and assessment methods.

Evaluation involves conducting both formative and summative evaluations. The formative evaluation process really begins in the analysis stage and then reoccurs as the course is run over and over. Summative evaluation takes place at milestones during course delivery and at the end. Feedback from all the evaluations feeds back into the appropriate phase for adjustment and improvement.

CONCLUSION

GOOD INSTRUCTIONAL DESIGN comes from a thoughtful examination of the needs analysis and an assessment of who the learners will be and what their backgrounds are. These data are used to create good learning delivery choices for content that aligns with the needs analysis requirements. The design needs to include a course assessment, and instructor feedback needs to be incorporated. Finally the instructional design needs to include a process for course evaluation to enable future improvements.

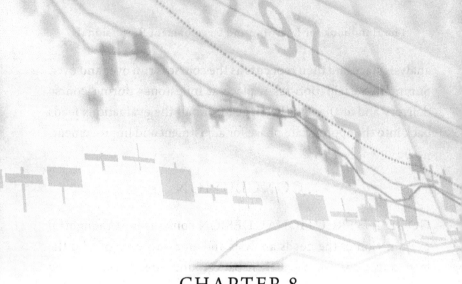

CHAPTER 8

Teaching and Coaching

INTRODUCTION

ARE TEACHING AND coaching the same? I think we can agree that teaching is providing instruction to enable another person to learn new knowledge or expand upon their present knowledge of a subject. It could also be providing instruction on how to execute a skill. Coaching is also teaching, but it involves observation and feedback as well. Teaching does not necessarily include feedback or specific instruction based on the observation. It may, but this is not a requirement of teaching. So, coaching is teaching, but teaching is not necessarily coaching.

This chapter will outline different approaches to teaching and coaching. Several, and perhaps even all, of these approaches may be applied in teaching a multiday course. Depending on the topic to be taught, the students, the location, and so on, all these elements play into which approach is the best choice. Having a good understanding of each approach leads to better course delivery, design, and planning.

DISCOVERY-BASED APPROACH TO INSTRUCTION

IN THIS APPROACH, the learning starts off by giving the students a problem to solve. The students then attempt to solve the problem, typically in small groups. This really allows the students to become engaged in the learning. They will solve some aspects and struggle with others, but they will come to have a deep sense of what they need to learn in order to overcome the problem. Once the students have reached this point, the teacher gives the chalk-and-talk teaching lesson. The students are then given the same type of problem, but with different variables. Coaching is then used to help the students successfully conquer the problem.

We're starting to see this approach used in K–12 schools, where it has been met with varying degrees of success. It certainly has its critics who feel that lecture and practice, or good old rote learning, is the only way. But I do think discovery-based learning is becoming more widely accepted. One of the keys to the discovery-based approach is having students who are keen to learn, and this is quite often a matter of how relevant they find the topic. With K–12 or adult learners, as I've stated several times in *The Handbook for Learning and Development Professionals*, it is vital to establish the relevance of the topic. If learners do not find the topic of any relevance to them, then their motivation will be low to zero.

An example of this approach is when I worked at Dow Chemical. The plant operators learned how to weld as part of an operator maintenance program. Most of the students were excited to learn how to weld, and to be honest, most of them saw the relevance to their jobs but saw even greater relevance to home projects or "government jobs" as they liked to call them. Lawrence was our instructor, and he was a very experienced journeyman welder. He started by teaching all the safety aspects. Then he taught the operators about the equipment required, following which he showed them how to turn on the welder and how to hold the "stick." Then he laid a short bead. Next he gave them pieces of metal and said, "Go to your welders and weld these together." Sounds easy, right? Well, it turns out there are temperature settings on welders, and if they're not close to being set correctly, the welding process really doesn't work. On top of that, striking an arc with the stick and keeping the arc, and also making a good weld, takes knowledge and a lot of practice. Even if you know how to adjust the temperature settings, if you're not able to maintain an arc, there's no bead to analyze in order to adjust the temperature. The operators would strike an arc, and in less than a second the stick would stick to the metal. Not knowing if they were holding the stick the right distance away or at the right angle, or how to move it, was a big problem. Not knowing if the welder settings were right in the first place was another problem. Suffice it to say that they all struggled for about half an hour. Then Lawrence taught the operators about temperature settings, how to strike the arc, and what to look for, and they went back to the task with the confidence that they were on the right the track. Lawrence coached them along from that point. The discovery-based approach worked really well in this case.

The discovery-based teaching approach is a very good technique if it's used in the right situation with the right (highly motivated) students, and if a wise choice is made for the initial problem. Recognizing when to use this approach and what problem to include in the design comes from knowledge, experience, and practice applying the discovery-based approach. Don't be afraid to try it if you feel the topic is one your students will be highly motivated to master. Have a backup plan for teaching the topic. If the discovery-based approach is not making progress and the students are showing signs that their determination is turning into frustration, you need to be able to seamlessly switch to an alternative approach.

SOCIAL CONNECTION TO LEARNING

LEARNING IS A social activity. Emotional and social dimensions related to online learning do have an influence on a student's learning, according to Wosnitza and Volet (2005). Other research into distance learning shows that learning at a distance can result in being disconnected socially, which is a hindrance to learning. Specifically, it can result in transactional distance, which is the psychological distance that is created between the learner and the teacher. The gap is in communication and social connection, which leads to two-way miscommunication between student and teacher (Moore 2013).

Whether the lesson is being taught at a distance or face-to-face, it's important to understand the social connection. As an instructor, you'll be more effective if you develop a social connection with your learners. A good way of developing this connection with learners is always to use their first names as this recognizes the importance of each student's individuality and will increase the effectiveness of your teaching. Another aspect of using first names is that it shows respect and helps to build a positive relationship with the learners. It is important to make individual connections with the learners.

You might be surprised to discover how many times you skip by an opportunity to call a student by his or her name. I know a few of my university professors did.

Student name plaques are a common sight. You walk into a workplace classroom session and there are always name plaques and a marker for you to fill in your name. There's nothing wrong with this, but I would recommend using the name cards to memorize the students' names as quickly as possible, as there's much less of an individual connection if the instructor looks down at the name card first then calls the student by name. If early in a session the instructor doesn't have to look at the name cards, this will build rapport sooner. If you are not good at remembering names (I am not), the key to remember is to show respect for the students and their contributions and to look for any personal connections you can make.

COMMAND APPROACH TO INSTRUCTION

ALL THE VARIOUS approaches differ in terms of student involvement in making decisions. The command approach to instruction is at one end of this spectrum, where the instructor makes all the decisions. The instructor determines how long each lesson will be, how long practice will be, who will sit where, who answers questions, what specific tasks are to be used for practice, and for how long the lesson will last. The instructor also asks questions to test for understanding, and so on. With this approach, the student's role is to listen, take notes, follow the instructor's instructions, and execute specific practice tasks within the time allotted. In a nutshell, the instructor provides the stimulus and the students provide the response.

An example of where this type of approach is successfully

applied is in first aid training. The instructor typically gives a short lecture about a topic, such as dealing with a broken wrist, and then gives a demonstration of how to splint and immobilize a broken wrist. Next the instructor provides a certain amount of time for the students to practice on each other while the instructor moves from pair to pair to coach and advise the students on the quality of their work. With this type of lesson—and most safety courses are run this way—there is only one correct way of executing the various tasks. For these types of lessons, the command approach is effective and efficient. First aid training could be taught equally well or perhaps even better with different approaches, but not in as short a time.

TASK APPROACH TO INSTRUCTION

THE TASK APPROACH is similar to the command approach except that students are given a little more leeway in making some of the decisions. The students are free to assemble themselves as they see fit, unlike with the command approach, where pairs or groups of set numbers are arranged by the instructor. The first part of the lesson mirrors the command approach where the instructor provides the lesson. However, in this case, the students are freer to ask questions. The real difference takes place once the instruction is complete as the students are then free to decide if they wish to work in pairs, in groups, or alone, as well as what tasks to practice and how much time to spend on each task. The instructor coaches the students on whatever task(s) they have chosen to practice. As adults, we tend to have a very good idea of what we know and can do, which enables us to determine what we need to work on and improve.

An example of this approach would be where a manufacturer is providing a course to a company's millwrights on overhauling and repairing a compressor the company has purchased from the manufacturer. For the first couple of days the course would be on the theory, operation, construction, and overhaul procedures for the compressor. The third day would allow for the millwrights to have access to various components of the compressor and whole compressors for practicing. The millwrights would choose what they wanted to practice and for how long, while the instructor(s) would be available for help and answering questions.

INCLUSION APPROACH TO INSTRUCTION

IN THIS APPROACH, students self-assess their degree of mastery of a subject and then are able to enter the instruction at the level (place) of their choosing. Obviously not all subjects lend themselves to this approach, and there is also the issue of students being able to properly self-assess their level of knowledge. If you realize in developing a course that the students will have a wide range of knowledge and skills, this style is something to consider as you design the learning and teaching approach.

As an example of this, we'll say that company X has sixteen leadership courses, some of which are on topics covered by two or three courses that build on each other. This company has supervisors and managers who have come from other companies where they have already had various leadership training. In this situation, listing all the courses with thorough course descriptions allows each individual leader to determine the courses they need to take to continue their development, versus the courses for which they already have the required knowledge. Once students attend any of these sessions, the instructor needs to be aware that not all the students took the prerequisite course that company X offers, so the students will be coming into the sessions with slightly different levels of knowledge. A good approach for this type of arrangement is an overview course delivered online that covers the core knowledge needed to start the course.

SELF-CHECK APPROACH TO INSTRUCTION

AS THE NAME suggests, with this type of approach students self-assess their progress and mastery as they progress through a course or program. The instructor provides detailed criteria to the students, against which they can self-assess their mastery of the learning as they progress. This approach begins with a lesson from the instructor, anything from a lecture to online instruction or a blended-learning approach. Armed with this knowledge and instruction, the learners proceed with a self-check exercise using the provided criteria to assess their mastery and their ability to progress.

This approach typically lends itself to a hands-on type of competence. As an example, an air conditioning and heating mechanic may attend a course on how to perform certain repairs to an industrial air conditioner. The course would start with instruction on the theory of operation and maintenance of the unit, followed by how to safely execute certain repairs on the equipment. After this, the students would be supplied with repair instructions and criteria to use for assessing whether the repair is being completed properly. The students would then be provided with test units to perform the repairs on and would use the provided criteria to self-check that they've successfully completed each step and each repair properly. The instructor would roam the class, provide coaching, answer any student questions, and perhaps draw the entire class's attention to something brought up by a student.

PEER APPROACH TO INSTRUCTION

WITH THIS APPROACH, instruction is provided first, in the form of face-to-face learning, distance learning, or blended learning. Once the students have the requisite knowledge, they are paired up. One student (A) is provided with the criteria for successfully executing the task(s) while the other student (B) performs the task(s). While student B is executing the task(s), student A provides feedback. This approach lends itself to the social aspect of learning between learners. It allows for a great deal of feedback and enables the instructor to observe all pairs and provide individual coaching where required.

I've seen this approach used successfully in self-contained breathing apparatus (SCBA) training. For those of you unfamiliar with SCBA, these are the tanks you see firefighters wearing on their backs, supplying fresh breathing air so the firefighters can go where there's not enough oxygen to support life, like a smoke-filled burning house. SCBA is not to be confused with SCUBA, which is similar but is used for going under water. SCBA doesn't work under water, but I digress. In this training, the instructor teaches the students all about the SCBA and demonstrates donning and doffing of the equipment. Students then pair off, and while one dons the SCBA, the other student with the criteria on hand ensures his or her partner is doing everything properly and in the correct sequence. Then the two students reverse roles. Once they've both donned and doffed the SCBA enough times to be confident they can do it properly without any help or feedback, they summon the instructor, who evaluates their mastery of donning and doffing the SCBA equipment.

DIVERGENT DISCOVERY APPROACH TO INSTRUCTION

IN THIS APPROACH the student is given a question that she must develop an answer for. Typically it's the type of question that has multiple answers. For example, at the end of the first day of a two- or three-day course on air compressor repair and overhaul training, the instructor may give all the students a failure symptom of the compressor that could be caused by a number of things. At the start of the next day the students present their causes for the symptom, which leads into a class discussion on each possible cause. Several students likely will have the same cause for the symptom. If any possibilities are missed, the instructor puts them forth for discussion. This is a very good approach as it makes the students do some high-level thinking and learning (see Bloom's taxonomy in chapter 7). It also creates good, involved discussion, which aids the social aspect of learning that is very important.

GUIDED DISCOVERY APPROACH TO INSTRUCTION

WITH THIS APPROACH the students are given a series of questions, either a sequence that needs to be worked through in order or a series of questions that, once answered, lead to learning something. This approach can be embedded in a larger teaching scenario. For example, I use this approach with a section of a course I developed for people to become competency validators within the oil and gas industry. As preparatory work for the course, I give the students three dates of disasters on which to do an internet search. They are told they will need to be able to provide a short presentation on what happened and what was learned from the disaster. This leads to good class discussion around what the industry learned and how industry reacted and implemented the learning. What the students learn leads in to the rest of course. With the discovery type of instruction, there is a high level of student engagement, which has a high influence on the students' learning. I find that these approaches fit into many course designs as small embedded sections. I have always had very good success with students having successful learning sessions involving discovery approaches, which then carry over into the larger topic of instruction.

USING HUMOR

PART OF MY bachelor of education degree required I do student teaching. I was lucky to be able to work under the guidance of an amazing high school teacher, Phil Quinn. Phil taught math and physical education. At the start of every math class, Phil would tell a joke; this was a big hit with the students. I came to find out that everything Phil did was well thought out and planned to aid in teaching his students. There has been research done and books written in the area of humor and its connections to learning environments (Cornett 1986; Leacock 1937). Humor, especially when it is funny enough to create laughter, produces a number of notable effects. It supports bonding, which in turn creates comfort, leading to the lowering of barriers. Another extension of the bonding aspect of sharing a laugh is that it helps to create a nonthreatening atmosphere. These are all positive characteristics of a good learning environment. It relieves stress and tension, and it makes muscles relax. Have you ever noticed that you cannot lift something heavy and laugh at the same time? A good learning environment is low on the stress and tension scale. Humor and laughter refresh the brain, helping to clear it for thinking and learning. Phil knew this and leveraged this tactic to help his students. All the students knew was that they liked his class.

The jokes Phil told to start his classes were mostly found in *Reader's Digest*. Through the course of each class Phil would convey a few humorous comments. What is humor? How does it work? Humor is pretty much based on a twist or a surprise, the punch line that comes at the end. Take for example the play-on-words approach: "An officer asked me if my dog had a license. I said, 'No, I do all the driving.'" The last word, *driving*, provides the surprise twist. Another humor strategy is the reverse approach: "I've been doing so much reading on the evils of drinking, I've given up reading." With the implication approach, the strategy is not about what you say but what's embedded in it. The humor can be in the conclusion the receiver comes to: there are three things I can never remember ... Humor can be created by forming a visual for the receiver or describing a funny situation, which is best conveyed by mentally painting the image of what makes the scene funny at the very end.

Humor is a double-edged sword, however. Anything that is funny is bound to be offensive to someone somewhere. I once tried only making fun of myself while teaching a course, but I quickly found out there are people who will be offended on my behalf. Honestly, there are things that offend me every day, but it is rare that anything will cause me to react outwardly. I think it is good to have different emotions throughout the day, and being offended is one of them. In this area, things are different than they were ten or more years ago, and this poses a challenge. Humor is clearly beneficial in a learning environment, but even seemingly innocuous humor can be taken as hurtful and offensive by some.

If you are going to use humor, know your students. Jordan Peterson (2018) states that blue-collar workers have a different sense of humor than white-collar workers do. I can attest to this, having worked in both environments. There are some courses that I teach to both blue-collar workers based out in the field and to

white-collar workers at the head office in the city. For these courses,
I actually have two different versions. The only difference is in the
humorous elements that are included. For blue-collar field workers
I use more humor, and while it is tame, it is more edgy than what
I can use at the head office with white-collar workers. I've had
complaints about some of the material being offensive from some
white-collar workers. I've never had any blue-collar workers be
offended. Interestingly the courses in the field that contain more
humor have much better class participation throughout the course.
I attribute this to the positive effects of humor. All I can offer for
advice is that if you choose to use humor as I do, learn your audience
and be careful.

CONCLUSION

THE MORE AN instructor can involve the students and have
them participate in the learning, the better. Some subjects are more
conducive to high student involvement, whereas some topics and
situations call for the lecture and practice type of approach. In this
chapter the common approaches to instruction were described, but
ultimately it is up to the instructor and instructional design team to
use the approach they deem best given the environment, students,
and topic. Lastly, when teaching and coaching, use humor where
you can.

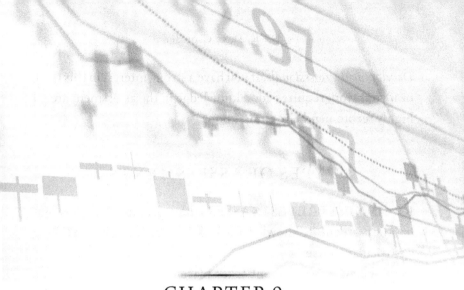

CHAPTER 9

Student Assessment

INTRODUCTION

ASSESSMENT OF STUDENT achievement is a wide-ranging category with a multitude of approaches and methods for determining the degree to which students are achieving learning objectives. A well-designed and well-implemented assessment program will lead to more effective instruction and thereby higher student achievement. This chapter will discuss the terminology, cover the more common approaches, and provide practical examples.

Years back I read the book *Assessment of Student Achievement* by Norman E. Gronlund (1998). It shaped my thinking and experience in this area. The research I have read, and all my practical experience, aligns directly with the teachings in *The Handbook for Learning and*

Development Professionals. If you have a strong interest in this field, or if your work requires good knowledge in the assessment area, I highly recommend Gronlund's book.

TYPES OF ASSESSMENTS

READINESS PRETESTS ASSESS the degree to which a student has the prerequisite knowledge and skills to be successful in taking a particular course.

Formative assessment takes place during the course. This type of assessment can take the form of formal tests or may be as simple as the instructor asking questions during instruction and checking that the class has understood what was just taught. The results from formative assessments are then fed back into improving the instruction. For example, if the instructor asks students a question about what was just taught and the students struggle with answering some aspects, the instructor then explains those elements again, possibly with a different approach. The instructor does not just move on to the next lesson. The instructor should then note any and all areas of difficulty and make needed adjustments the next time he or she instructs that section. Likewise, information derived from written or online tests during instruction (formative) must be applied to make adjustments to instruction and ensure the learning objectives are achieved by all.

Diagnostic assessment probes deeper than formative assessment. This type of assessment typically uses a large number of questions and employs slight variations in the questions to pinpoint specific learning errors.

Summative assessment takes place at the end of a course and is focused on how well the students achieved (learned) the intended outcomes of the course. Typically a summative assessment is a final exam or assignment with the results used for grading purposes. Even so, feedback based on the results should be given to the students. Furthermore, the data gained from the summative assessment is used to evaluate the effectiveness of the instruction and is applied to improve future courses.

Selection-type tests (selected response) include true–false, multiple choice, and matching an answer to a description. A common belief is that only low-level knowledge testing can be done with this type of test. While this is typically the case, a well-designed multiple-choice test can be used to assess learning at the highest levels, unless of course you're testing for writing ability. My point is, I wouldn't shy away from this type of test. It is quickly administered, it can easily be done online, and it provides instant valuable feedback to the learner.

Supply-type tests (supply response) require the students to reply with a response of their own creation and choosing. This would typically be a word, phrase, or even an essay response. We are all familiar with this approach from our years in traditional school. However, this type of test could also be made up of questions given in a field situation, in which a trainee may be required to go on a walk-through with a validator to answer questions and describe the equipment he or she will be expected to be able to operate or repair.

Performance-type assessments (competency assurance validations) are used to assess a student's performance in demonstrating a task or competency. A specific list of criteria would be determined, and the student would be evaluated against it. This could range from public speaking to repairing a multistage centrifugal compressor—or anything in between.

Guidelines for Effective Student Assessment

1. Have a clear conception of what all the intended learning outcomes are. The assessments must be geared toward each of them.

2. Use a variety of assessment approaches (if possible and if appropriate).
3. Consider the instructional relevance of the assessment approaches. Consider how each one will help the student and enable insight into the instruction for the purpose of improving it.
4. Find the balance between having an endless assessment that covers every little detail and an assessment that does not cover everything adequately. There is a fine line between testing enough and not testing enough.
5. The assessment procedures need to be fair for everyone. If the class has several students whose first language is different from that of the others, written assessments will put them at a disadvantage, and the assessment results will not be an accurate reflection of those students' overall achievement.
6. Have clear criteria for what is expected of the students. The students need to have an unambiguous view of what is expected of them.
7. Students need to receive feedback from the assessments. The feedback needs to be comprehensive, so a simple pass or fail is not enough. The feedback should be as immediate as possible, should indicate strengths and weaknesses, should be positive, and should focus on improvement.
8. If scoring is connected to the assessment, that scoring needs to be fair and consistent.

Testing Theory—Planning

The following steps serve as a guide for developing a test:

1. Identify and define the intended learning outcomes to be assessed.

2. Prepare the test specifications, namely, criteria that describe the outcome that was learned.
3. Construct test times based on the determined criteria.
4. Review and edit test items. Pilot them if possible.
5. Arrange the constructed items in the form of the chosen test type.
6. Prepare directions for completing the test.

In determining what type of assessment to develop, you can categorize learning into two cognitive domains. The first is knowledge, as in knowledge of facts, terms, principles, and theories. The second is intellectual abilities and skills. These are defined as

- comprehension—understanding the meaning;
- application—being able to apply knowledge in real situations;
- analysis—understanding relationships, principles, and their purpose;
- synthesis—understanding all the parts and how they interact; and
- evaluation—knowledge and ability to make judgments in terms of internal and external evidence (troubleshooting errors).

Once you've determined the level of testing and precisely what should be tested and how, consider how long the duration of the test should be. Do you have any time constraints that need to be considered? Is the topic of high technical or safety importance? Adult students understand that testing, especially with respect to regulatory requirements, is necessary, but they still don't like tests. You have to weigh the need and requirements against the necessity.

CONSTRUCTING MULTIPLE-CHOICE TESTS

MULTIPLE-CHOICE QUESTIONS CAN be used to measure learning outcomes from the simple to the complex.

Example:

A baseball game consists of how many innings? (This is the stem/question.)

Distractors ⎯ { a) 5
b) 7
c) 6
d) 9 } ⎯ Alternatives (options or choices)

The larger the number of choices, the more accurate the results, provided each distractor is plausible. Typically, multiple-choice tests are used to measure if the student has grasped the material without having to apply it. The tests measure if students understand the meaning—do they understand the concept, do they understand the terms associated with the concept, and do they understand the effects of an action relating to the concept?

An example of a multiple-choice question for measuring a more complex learning outcome is as follows:

What trend would you expect see if_____?

This requires the learner to be able to apply the comprehension knowledge she has and deduce an outcome from cause-and-effect thinking based on the concept in question.

Tips for Writing Multiple-Choice Questions

- Design each question to measure a specific learning outcome.

- Ensure that the stem presents a clearly formulated problem. The student should understand the question without having to read the alternatives.
- State the stem in simple, clear language.
- Keep the alternative choices as short as possible; the stem can be as long as is necessary.
- Ensure the distractors are plausible and appealing.
- Avoid using choices such as "none of the above" or "all of the above." These almost always render the question less effective than if they were not used.
- Randomly vary the position of the correct answer.
- Ensure each question is independent of the other questions on the test. Be careful not to accidently give away clues to other questions.
- Follow the rules of grammar. If the stem is a question ending in a question mark, then each alternative should start with a capital letter and end with a period.
- Do not repeat words in each of the alternative choices.
- State the stem in a positive tone. Ask "What is the best …?" not "What is the poorest …?"
- If negative wording must be used, do something to emphasize it. Put words in italics or underline them, or both. "Why should you *not* mix chemicals X and Y?"
- Ensure the intended answer is correct and is clearly the best response.
- Make all the alternatives grammatically consistent with the stem.
- Avoid verbal clues that could enable the student to choose the correct answer or eliminate any of the other choices. Watch for repeating words from the stem or using greater conciseness and/or clarity in the correct alternative.

TRUE–FALSE TESTS

IF THERE ARE only two possible alternatives, then a true–false question is the most appropriate choice.

Tips for Writing True–False Questions:

- Statements of opinion should be referenced to their source, unless they are used to distinguish between fact and opinion.
- When cause–effect relationships are being measured, use only true propositions.
- Avoid including accidental clues as to the answer. Qualifiers with absolutes such as *always, never, all, none,* and *only* tend be false. Qualifiers such as *usually, may,* and *sometimes* tend to be true.
- When measuring more complex learning outcomes, base the questions on the introductory material.
- Use only one central idea in each question.
- Keep the questions short, and use straightforward vocabulary and sentence structure.
- Word the statement precisely; the student must be able to unequivocally judge the question as true or false. Avoid vague terms such as *may, like, possible, seldom, often,* and *frequently.*
- Avoid the use of negative words and wording (double negatives). The words *no* and *not* are often overlooked, especially by a student under the pressure of a test.

INTERPRETIVE EXERCISES

IN THESE TESTS, an introductory diagram, chart, series of graphs (trends), schematic, or such is provided. Then a series of multiple-choice and/or true–false questions are asked in reference to the supplied graphic. For example, an electrical drawing with certain voltages and resistances and other pertinent electrical data is shown, and then troubleshooting questions are asked. This type of test is good for measuring complex learning objectives. Make sure to use familiar but new introductory material, and align the questions to the learning objectives.

MATCHING ITEMS TESTS

WHEN IT BECOMES apparent that the same alternatives will be repeated and/or will be used in several multiple-choice questions, use a matching items question. Follow these basic guidelines:

- Include only related material in each matching question.
- Keep the list of items short, ten items or less.
- Use a larger or smaller number of responses than the premises and permit the responses to be used more than once. Be clear in letting the student know a response can be used more than once.
- Place the brief response descriptions on the right-hand side.
- Put the selection items in alphabetical order.
- Be careful formatting the test if it is hard copy; you want to ensure all the descriptions and matches are on the same page.

SHORT-ANSWER TEST QUESTIONS

THESE QUESTIONS REQUIRE the student to answer a question with one word or a few sentences.

Tips for Writing Short-Answer Questions

- Ensure the question is precise enough to result in the intended correct response.
- For fill-in-the-blank questions, ensure the blank relates directly to the main point of the statement.
- Do not use more than one blank in a question, as multiple blanks become confusing. The only exception is for two related answers, for example, "Litmus paper is used to measure the pH of <u>acids</u> and <u>bases</u>."
- Word the statement so the blank appears at the end of the statement.
- Avoid using the word *a* or *an* just before a blank as it can provide clues to the answer.

ESSAY QUESTIONS

I WON'T SPEND much time on these questions because they are rarely used in industry and corporate learning. Essay questions are the best way to measure complex learning objectives, and they allow the student the greatest freedom to respond with his or her own creativity. Responses are expected to provide reasons, explanations, interpretation of data, and cohesive, well-formulated conclusions. As the students have a great deal of liberty in answering an essay question, consider stating some limits and boundaries to keep the answer more focused.

Essays can be difficult to grade. Similar to competency

validations (chapter 18), create a list of criteria the essay should address, and be sure the question leads to these criteria being addressed in the essay, as this creates a grading key for assessing an essay.

CONCLUSION

ASSESSMENTS WILL AID student motivation. They provide short-term goals for students to focus on and help to clarify what is to be learned. Finally, they provide feedback to the students on their progress. All these things help the student's motivation. Assessments allow the instructor and the student to measure the student's progress. Assessments provide information for the purposes of adjusting and improving the learning instruction and content. Several types of assessments can be chosen from, and each needs to be carefully constructed.

Assessment results need to be forwarded back to the students as quickly as possible. This is an advantage of online multiple-choice tests. As soon as the student completes a test, he gets immediate results, and he can then reflect on his mistakes and, in his mind, correct the errors he made. It enables students to quickly clear misconceptions they may have. When students get a test back a week or more later, they cannot remember what they were thinking and how they arrived at certain answers. This is particularly important for those answers the student got correct but struggled with and for those the student answered incorrectly. Immediate feedback is a powerful aid to learning.

All assessments should be examined to determine where there are weaknesses in the instruction. If one area of assessment shows lack of learning by the students more than other areas, obviously improvements should be made. It may require a different approach for the instruction in that area, or it may simply require that more time be spent on that area. Similarly, if there's an area the students are excelling in, that area of instruction should be examined to see if it can be shortened.

The following questions are considerations in designing an assessment:

- Will it improve student motivation?
- Will it enable improved student performance?
- Will it encourage learning in this area beyond the formal learning provided?
- Will its use enhance self-assessment abilities?
- Will it aid in course improvements?
- Will it have a negative effect on the students or instruction?

CHAPTER 10

Program and Course Evaluation

INTRODUCTION

IT IS VITALLY important for any learning and development department to be able to demonstrate its value to the organization. The better a learning and development team can convey their worth, the better position they are in to compete for the resources they need to effectively execute their role in the organization. Results from a program evaluation also help the learning and development team to know what to improve on, what can be dropped, what needs to be reconsidered, and what, if any, lacuna exists. In most organizations, the only formalized evaluation that takes place consists of forms (commonly referred to as surveys or smile sheets) that are filled out by participants at the end of a course. While a properly designed end-of-course evaluation form provides valuable data, it is only part of a comprehensive evaluation program.

There are several approaches for evaluating programs and courses. It has been my experience that Kirkpatrick's model is the best known and most used. I've seen more than one author change a few minor things in the model and rename a few more, and then pass it off as their own evaluation process. I understand that is considered a form of flattery, though I'll just give Dr. Kirkpatrick the credit up front. I highly recommend Donald Kirkpatrick's book *Evaluating Training Programs: The Four Levels* (1998).

KIRKPATRICK'S EVALUATION MODEL

KIRKPATRICK DEVELOPED HIS evaluation model to evaluate training programs (1959a, 1959b, 1960a, 1960b, 1998). Kirkpatrick's evaluation method uses four levels to evaluate the effectiveness of learning courses and programs, labeled as reaction, learning, behavior, and results. Each level's evaluation has an influence on the next, and the levels become increasingly more difficult to measure as the evaluation process progresses up through the levels (Kirkpatrick 1998).

Before getting to the four levels, we need to examine the foundation the evaluations will be based upon. Kirkpatrick (1998) states that an evaluation of a learning program should be done to determine its effectiveness. Effectiveness of learning is defined as the degree to which the learning program contributes to learner success. Considerable forethought and planning should be put into the development of a learning program in order to create as effective a program as possible from the outset. Start with the planning and implementing stages, during which the following factors should be considered:

1. learning needs analysis
2. definition of learning objectives
3. what should be included in the learning content
4. determination of the target audience
5. consideration of what schedule will work best and how technology can be used advantageously to make scheduling of learning more flexible
6. making the best choices of instructors/facilitators
7. selection of the learning aids and technology to be used
8. the administration aspects of coordinating the program
9. evaluation of the program

I discussed learning needs analysis in chapter 5, so I will not go into depth here when relating it to an evaluation program. For a learning program to be effective, it must meet the needs of the learners. There are several ways to determine the learning needs. One of these methods or a combination of the methods could be used: (a) the prospective students could be surveyed, (b) the students' superiors could articulate what they see as the needs, (c) others who are very familiar with the needs of the students could provide input, or (d) the learning may be dictated by a regulatory body. Testing, or some type of performance analysis, could be performed to determine the gaps that a learning program could fill (Kirkpatrick 1998). There is no point in doing an evaluation if there is not a clear understanding of what the program is trying to accomplish. Proper needs analysis is the foundation of many aspects of a solid learning and development program.

Learning objectives are established once the needs of the learners have been ascertained. The objectives are set to handle three aspects of learning (Kirkpatrick 1998). First, what knowledge, skills, and/or attitudes do the students need to acquire? Next, what results are expected from the learning? Finally, what are the results that the learning is expected to produce?

The learning content is designed to meet the learning objectives. Subsequently, the learning content will determine what topics should be covered. Knowing the topics and the depth to which they need to be covered guides not only the learning content and instructional design but also the level of qualification required by the presenter/instructor (Kirkpatrick 1998).

Kirkpatrick (1998) discusses four questions to ask regarding the selection of participants:

1. Who could benefit from the learning?
2. Is the course required by law or a regulatory body?
3. Should this learning be compulsory or voluntary?
4. Is there a need to segregate students for any reason?

Having the content specifically designed for this target audience will result in the participants benefiting the most from what they learn. It will also enable a better evaluation to be executed, as the evaluation can focus very specifically on learning objectives that were designed with a targeted purpose. The clearer and more detailed the program design, the better the focus of the evaluation will be.

In determining the best schedule for delivering the training, Kirkpatrick (1998) identifies three concerns to take into consideration: (a) a schedule that is the best for the teacher, (b) a schedule that best suits the students, and (c) the best conditions for learning. He also identifies a preference for spreading a course out over time to provide maximum flexibility for everyone involved in the learning (Kirkpatrick 1998).

An important decision regarding conditions for learning is the selection of the learning facility. The learning environment should be convenient and comfortable for the learners. The furniture should be comfortable, the room should be of adequate size, the room temperature should be comfortable, and noise and other distractions should be minimized. There should be adequate breaks, and there should be access to food and beverages for the students, including choices that the students desire (Kirkpatrick 1998). While Kirkpatrick developed his model long before personal computers, handheld devices, and online learning came along, clearly these things can accommodate his criteria for scheduling, flexibility, and student comfort.

Selecting the appropriate instructors is critical to the success of the learning program. The instructors need to be good communicators, be motivated to teach, and be knowledgeable in the subject matter. The instructors should have a desire to meet the learners' needs and have a genuine desire to want to help the students (Kirkpatrick 1998).

While I was working for a multinational oil and gas company in the early 2000s, we were building a multibillion-dollar oil sand upgrader. Brian was the maintenance manager, and he knew he was going to be managing a budget of hundreds of millions of dollars a year. Keeping such a large department organized and doing maintenance in a cost-effective manner was going to be a challenge. Brian developed a strategic approach, a culture really, to how he wanted maintenance to be approached and executed with a strong emphasis on being proactive and focused on reliability. If equipment lasts longer, your repair and replacement costs go down. His strategy was a huge departure for most of the new employees from the way they had experienced maintenance organizations in the past. Brian needed to educate two hundred people on how this system was going to work and what everyone's roles and responsibilities would be within it. In our conversations, Brian realized that while he and his leadership team were passionate about this approach, it might be a tough sell to the rest of the maintenance team, who were not familiar with this type of strategy. Having strong buy-in is important for learner motivation as it was ultimately for Brian's new approach to be successful.

We took a lesson from Kirkpatrick. We needed instructors who were knowledgeable, good communicators, motivated to teach, and willing to go that extra mile for the learners. While members of our L & D team had the instructor skills and could learn the material and deliver it, we went a different direction on this. For instructors, we chose to go with using Brian himself and then select members of his leadership team as they knew the material and they were passionate about it. And this energy was instrumental to teaching and getting buy-in on the learning. I worked with Brian and his team to develop the instructional design and to determine who on his team were the best candidates to teach which parts. The course was very successful—sure, the course design and activities were good, but it was really the instructors that made it. Not to mention, here was a senior manager taking time to teach part of the course, and he had his leadership guys teaching too. The shop floor people and operators knew Brian was 100 percent behind it, and they respected his direct involvement. My point is, the best choice for instructors is not always people from the L & D group with teaching experience. Wherever possible, a shared collaborative approach should be considered.

Teaching aids such as audiovisuals should be used to communicate and maintain interest. They can be used to create interest and entertain as well. An entire learning program can be an audiovisual package (Kirkpatrick 1998). A humorous YouTube-type video related to a learning lesson can be a great way to kick off a learning session as it lightens the mood and allows the instructor to describe the learning at a high level while making references to the video. I try to use humorous videos throughout a lesson as long as they are relevant to the topic being taught/discussed. I really like videos that help to stimulate interest in the students, but these are typically harder to find. Naturally, if you can find a video that explains a topic well, it's a great option to supplement the instruction.

Level 4 Results (ROI)	The degree to which the application of the learning by the students results in positive gains

Level 3 Behavior Change	The degree to which the students apply their learning back on the job

Level 2 Learning	The degree to which the students acquire the intended knowledge, skills, and/or change in attitude (confidence)

Level 1 Reactions	The degree to which the students react favorably to the learning event

Level 1

Level 1 of the process evaluates reaction. Reactions are a measure of the participant's response to everything about the learning intervention. Reaction feedback is important because it provides comments and suggestions for improving the learning. It sends the message to the learners that the instructors care and desire feedback to help them improve their teaching and the program. It provides data showing the level of learner satisfaction with the content and delivery. The data from the reactions can be used to set standards for how well future learning should be received. Reaction feedback is typically gathered via survey sheets shortly after the learning program concludes (Kirkpatrick 1959a, 1998). Kirkpatrick (1998) provides the following considerations for reaction surveys:

1. Determine what it is you want to find out. This will help you focus your questions.
2. Design a survey form that will quantify the results you seek.
3. Encourage written feedback (comments and suggestions).
4. Have the participants complete their reaction survey form immediately at the end of the course.
5. Get a 100 percent participation rate, versus sampling.
6. Keep reaction surveys anonymous so as to encourage honest feedback.
7. Use the results to improve the program.

It is important not to take this step lightly. Considerable thought and effort should be put into developing a level 1 reaction survey. As Pasquale (2009) states, the reaction level cannot take into account all the variables that influence the end results. If you are going to get a clear picture of why your program did or did not achieve its desired outcomes, the level 1 evaluation needs to come as close as possible to taking into account all the variables influencing the learning. This takes considerable forethought and effort.

While I was working at one company, the learning and development people were spread out in offices throughout a very large main administration building, and we had no dedicated training room. We had to use various conference rooms for training courses, none of which were designed for learning sessions, so we had to use a portable projector, a laptop, and plug-in speakers. When an opportunity arose for us to take over a small area of the administration building that included a good-sized conference room we could convert to a purpose-built training room, we jumped at the chance to make our bid for the area. We were in competition with other departments who also had good reasons for wanting the space. I made our bid and was successful because I had a large stack of level 1 evaluation forms filled out by students in the previous two years. These evaluations were all positive except in the area of feedback regarding the learning facilities, which were quite negative in contrast. In seeing that data, the general manager was convinced this was an area we could, and needed to, improve on. As I said, the L & D team got the space.

Level 2

Level 2 evaluates learning, which is a measure of how much change occurred in the participants' knowledge and skill levels, based on the learning objectives, and/or if a change in attitude resulted. In level 3, no change in behavior can be expected if none of the learning objectives were reached in level 2. This is why it is important to measure learning first and then measure the behavior (Kirkpatrick 1959b, 1998). Kirkpatrick (1998) provides the following considerations for measuring learning:

1. Determine if it is practical to use a control group.
2. Use before tests and after tests to measure learning.
3. Use a written test to assess knowledge and/or attitude change.
4. Use a performance test to measure skill change.
5. Get a 100 percent participation rate, versus sampling.
6. Use the results to improve the program.

Level 3

Level 3 evaluates the extent to which a person's behavior changed as a result of the learning intervention. Behavior change, or taking action as a result of the learning, is the most important outcome of a learning program. It is important not to skip level 1 and level 2 evaluations and jump directly to a level 3 evaluation. The participants may have positive reactions to the learning, and they may have gained a great deal of knowledge and skill, but a learner's behavior may not change because of barriers in the situation where he or she is expected to apply the learning.

At one company, my team put together a great learning package for plant process operators on performing energy isolation. This is a process that is followed to ensure a plant system is safe for maintenance to work on. When it is completed properly, no form of hazardous energy exists (e.g., chemical, heat, electrical). The learning package started with an online course to teach the knowledge component, then we had a classroom/workshop session that simulated an energy isolation. The level 1 evaluations were very positive. The participants passed the testing of their knowledge with flying colors (level 2). However, one of my team members who was charged with doing a level 3 evaluation received feedback that the operators were still performing energy isolation the old way and had not changed their behavior to execute the isolations the way we had instructed. After a little investigating, we determined that the software the operators had to use to execute the new isolation process had several issues that prevented the operators from using it in the field to perform the energy isolations. Levels 1 and 2 both passes, level 3 failed because of an unforeseen barrier. This is why you do a level 3 evaluation, to ensure there are no barriers to applying the learning. In this case the response to the training was positive, and the operators all gained the necessary knowledge, but a software issue created a barrier preventing the learners from applying their new knowledge. It is important to know where to focus an investigation if the behavior change does not occur (Kirkpatrick 1960a, 1998).

Kirkpatrick (1998) provides the following considerations for measuring behavior change:

1. If it is practical to do so, use a control group.
2. Test for behavior change before and after the learning.
3. Allow time for the change.
4. Interview and/or survey those in a position to observe the change.
5. Get a 100 percent participation rate, versus sampling.

Level 4

Level 4 evaluates results, identified as a measure of the positive benefits that came about as a result of the learning intervention. A level 4 evaluation is the most difficult of the four levels to measure. It is not easy to determine the tangible benefits of a learning program because in many cases evidence that can be accepted as hard proof cannot be gathered (Kirkpatrick 1960b, 1998). Yet this is the evaluation data business leaders want, and these leaders are the ones who hold the purse strings. This type of data clearly demonstrates a learning and development team's value, but it is very difficult to procure. Kirkpatrick (1998) provides the following considerations for measuring results:

1. If it is practical to do so, use a control group.
2. Allow for enough time for the results to show.
3. If it is practical to do so, measure before and after.
4. If proof doesn't exist, be satisfied with just evidence.

Kirkpatrick (1998) says that level 4 of his evaluation model is the most difficult to measure and that the practitioner may need to accept evidence to support the claim that the learning was responsible for an improvement as proof may not be possible to obtain. Stokking (1996) agrees, saying that getting a quality level 4 measurement is difficult because learning is not the only relevant causal factor. Yet this is the evaluation that data business leaders who control the money want to see. This type of data clearly demonstrates a learning and development team's value, but it can be very difficult to obtain.

Go Beyond Level 2

My experience in industry has been that an organization, for any number of reasons, becomes sold on the idea that a particular training is beneficial. If the training is delivered and the first two evaluation levels result in positive outcomes, the trust is there that the learning will be applied and there will be a positive return on investment (ROI) or an improvement in safety performance. The time and resources typically are not there to follow through with a good level 4 evaluation. That said, following are a couple of real-life examples of level 4 evaluations that did not take a great deal of time and effort:

In preparing maintenance tradesmen to be ready for maintaining a heavy oil refinery upon start-up, we identified a particular type of pump that could be problematic and determined our tradesmen should get specialized training on these pumps. In talking with the manufacturer, we learned that they did not offer training but thought it was a good idea and something they should offer. We partnered up, and they provided the technical expertise while I provided the learning expertise and coaching for their instruction. After they'd delivered their new course to our tradesmen, they delivered the course to another nearby company who also used their pumps. The other company had roughly the same number of pumps we had. If I remember correctly, we had forty-one and they had thirty-nine. In our first year we spent approximately $30,000 on parts for repairing these pumps. The other company the manufacturer provided training for also spent approximately $30,000 in the year following the training. However, prior to the training, for a number of years the other company had spent approximately $170,000 per year on parts to repairs those pumps. This is strong evidence that had we not provided the training to our tradesmen, we would've spent about $170,000 instead of the $30,000 we did. This data was very convincing to the maintenance manager, whom I needed to bargain with every year at budget time.

On another occasion at a petrochemical plant, we had just installed a new process control along with making major changes to a couple of large industrial furnaces used to start a world-scale plant. It takes many hours to get these furnaces started and completely up and running; if the start-up fails, it results in hours of lost production (for each failed attempt). The plant had a lot of historical data from previous start-ups, including the original start-ups when everything was new. Prior to the start-up we developed computer simulation training of the furnace start-ups so the operators could practice using the new process control and interface. This was the first time the operators had been given computer simulation training. This was back in the early 1990s, so that was not surprising. After the start-up, we compared the past start-ups and the number of failed attempts they experienced with this start-up. We also asked the operators individually how many failed start-ups they felt the computer simulation training had prevented. Using a meta-analysis of the number sets, the historical data, and the operators' estimates, we determined the difference the simulator training had made. This provided a degree of validation and provided a reliable number of production hours the simulation had saved from being lost. This data demonstrated that the production gained from not having failed start-up attempts more than paid for the cost of the simulator and training time. Computer simulations have proven their merits in many industries. Computer simulation use has become so widespread that I think most chemical and oil and gas insiders would say it's an industry standard now.

CONCLUSION

L & D departments should have a consistent approach to evaluating program results. Arguably the most widely used approach is Kirkpatrick's evaluation model. His evaluation process has four levels. Level 1 measures participant reactions to everything about the learning intervention. Level 2 measures how much of a change resulted from the learning objectives in relation to the participants' knowledge level or skill level, and/or if a change in attitude resulted. Typically this would be measured by some kind of a test or skill demonstration. Level 3 is a measure of the extent to which a person's behavior changed as a result of applying the learning. Level 4 is a measure of the positive benefits that came about as a result of the learning being applied. These levels cannot be skipped, and they need to be performed sequentially. Level 4 is the most difficult to perform, and direct evidence may not be possible to obtain.

CHAPTER 11

Ethical Practices in Learning and Development

INTRODUCTION

ETHICS IS SEEN as a much bigger issue for K–12 where children and authority figures are involved. It seems a month doesn't go by when one does not see a newspaper article about a high school teacher having inappropriate relations with a student. This is the extreme end of ethics and teaching. Typically it's smaller transgressions that occur in workplace learning. While they may seem small or petty, they have a real impact on the student and his or her learning. This chapter will cover a number of concepts relating to ethical behavior and then explain how these apply to teaching.

For example, I audited a train-the-trainer course for delivering team training. As part of this three-day course, the students, a group of about twelve heavy-duty maintenance workers, were made to play musical instruments and sing. None of these guys played any musical instrument, and none were singers—and they all knew it. Nor would it be common to find many in this type of demographic who would play musical instruments and/or sing. The number would certainly be less than 5 percent, though none of these workers would frown on a coworker who could play or sing. The group on average is just not that into the arts. When these guys were forced to play and sing, you could feel the tension. These guys were embarrassed but trying not to show it; they were uncomfortable, and you could see it. In a debrief with the instructors afterward, I brought up that the students were noticeably uncomfortable with that particular exercise and suggested it should be dropped. I was told the vendor's opinion was that this not only was an acceptable exercise but also that it served a valuable purpose, that being that people need to get out of their comfort zone to learn. Save that thought—I'll come back to it later. First let us look at some basic foundations of ethics or of being ethical.

VALUES

VALUES ARE DEFINED as the intergenerational cultural perspectives on matters of consequence. Values tend to cluster within ethnic groups and across generations of people who share a common history and geographic identity. Ultimately they are the basis for justifying one's actions in moral or ethical terms (Green and Kreuter 1991). Ethics are how we resolve issues when values are in conflict. Ethical theory, then, is how we explain our reasoning to solve these issues where our values are in conflict. Values are traditionally derived from three areas: religion, philosophy, and personal life.

MORAL CODE

IN THE WORLD today, there is no agreed-upon moral code or shared, agreed-to values. This a result of the many different cultures and religions, and this applies even within a single country. Two threats stemming from pluralism and uncertainty need to be considered. The first of these is relativism, that is, the view that all judgments about right or wrong, and evil or good, are only valid for certain societies or certain people or at certain times. The second is subjectivism, the view that all judgments about right or wrong, and evil or good, are not objective facts but rather subjective expressions of feelings and emotions and/or preferences and desires.

An ethical dilemma is a conflict among values that poses a problem in making a decision based on a standard of fairness, justice, rightness, goodness, and responsibility. It's a decision that cannot produce satisfactory outcomes given all the values involved. Consequentialism is an approach where the ethical decision is guided by the goal of achieving the best balance of good outcomes and the least sacrifice of important values. You may have heard of the principle of benefit maximization. This principle comes out of consequentialism, where we base the ethical decision on which decision benefits the most people or provides for the greatest benefit.

We often use substitutes to avoid genuine moral reasoning. We may do what feels right, but the problem with this is that what feels right might be exactly what's preventing a person from facing what needs to be done. Take for example blindly following the law. Laws are not based on ethical considerations. Many people broke the law to protect Jewish people from the Third Reich during World War II. It was illegal but ethical. Some religions forbid blood transfusions. What happens in the case where an eight-year-old child will die unless he receives a blood transfusion, but his family's religion forbids blood transfusions? At eight years of age, is a child competent to make a lifelong commitment to a religion, let alone a life-and-death decision based on a religion? Do the child's parents have the right to raise their child in the way they consider best, including religious beliefs? There are many different religions. Some forbid blood transfusions; others do not. Which religion is right? Regarding human rights, consider a pregnant woman whose health is at risk versus the right to life of the fetus. Whose rights are more important? Finally, in terms of following a code of ethics, the problem lies in that it can be interpreted in different ways, and no single code is able to address all the ethical issues that might arise. These are all reasons we cite for abdicating the problematic challenge of making ethical decisions.

SLIPPERY SLOPE

THE SLIPPERY SLOPE argument revolves around an ethical decision where the decision may be deemed ethical, but others worry it will become an accepted norm and thus pave the way to push the decision farther in that direction. Eventually, small step by small step, we arrive at a situation we would have never agreed to when the first decision (step) was made (taken). For example, we might decide obese people should pay more for health care, based on an argument that statistics show obese people are a greater burden on the health-care industry, so they should pay more. The slippery slope could mean eventually we'll apply the extra charge to anyone who does not have an ideal body mass index, and then to people who don't have an ideal diet, and so on.

KANE

AMERICAN PHILOSOPHER ROBERT Kane (2005) describes four levels of values. If you are presented with a situation where you have two extreme choices, rather than having to choose based on absolutes, you can choose the middle ground with respect to your values, Kane's four dimensions or levels allow this.

Level 1: Basic values are the experiences we have of delight, enjoyment, joy, amusement, love, ecstasy, a sense of accomplishment, and so on. Opposite to these we can experience pain, loneliness, despair, sadness, boredom, disappointment, humiliation, and so on. Since these basic feelings are essentially either good or bad, they can be characterized as values we have in that we would rather feel joy than sadness, for example. These values can be overridden by one of Kane's higher levels of values.

Level 2: Over time our lives involve purposive activities with goals and achievements, and through this we reach a second level of values. We acquire education; through accomplishing work we gain money and obtain houses and other possessions; we create art; we play games to win; and so on. These second-level values involve fulfilling a purpose, attaining a goal, and serving a particular function. These second-level values transcend the simpler first-level values in that the former are deeper and broader.

Level 3: These values come out of the significance and meaning of activities that stem from cultures, traditions, and the like. Patriotism, respect for authority, and performing rituals to mark life events are examples of third-level values. Note that these vary from culture to culture. Level 3 values go beyond our self-interest to our ideals. These values are subjective as they are determined and evaluated by human agents. Level 3 values are at a higher level than the others because they are the collective ideals of a larger group.

Level 4: This is the perspective of a value that is shared by all. Can there be values that everyone shares with equal reverence? As ethics are judgments on values, without the existence of a level 4 value, how can any ethical decision be just for all? Or is there a way to define a level 4 value?

RELATIVISM

RUNNING COUNTER TO Kane's fourth dimension, relativism's viewpoint is that ethical truths depend on the individual and the groups adhering to them. According to relativism, there are no objective, interpersonal, valid, ethical values. There are no universally shared values. Religions make attempts at creating universal values like those expressed by the Ten Commandments, and nations may do likewise, as with the American belief that everyone should be free to pursue life, liberty, and happiness. However, not all religions are Christianity, and many countries clearly do not believe their citizens should be free to pursue life, liberty, and/or happiness. But within particular groups there are shared universal values.

MODERNITY

MODERNITY CAME ABOUT in the seventeenth century. In this historical period of the Enlightenment, it was hoped that science would uncover objective truths and replace relativism. However, at the same time, exploration brought to light multiculturalism.

While science made great steps toward replacing relativism, multiculturalism did the opposite.

IMMANUEL KANT

KANT WAS A German philosopher who was born in 1724 and lived until 1804. He proposed that science and mathematics hold the key to making ethical decisions as they describe the world as it appears to us, and there is no interpretation (i.e., it is what it is). He reasoned that ethics and moral law should be arrived at through practical deliberation based on what we "ought" to do—in other words, what is best without regard for individual desires. Kant put forth two ethical imperatives:

1. Act only on that maxim which you can, and at the same time will that it should become a universal law.
2. Act so that you always use humanity in your own person, as well as the person of every other, never as a means, but at the same time an end.

Kant's view comes down to this: acts are judged good or bad, or right or wrong, based solely on themselves. By contrast, modern consequentialist ethical theory (utilitarianism) judges acts as good or bad, or right or wrong, based solely on the consideration of their consequences.

SOMEWHAT UNIVERSAL VALUE

THIS DISCUSSION BRINGS us back to our search for a universally accepted value or values. Perhaps the closest we've been able to come would be the physician's Hippocratic oath. There are many modern versions, but they all boil down to "Do no harm." This oath takes into account a number of considerations, including all the cultures, people, and subsequent values involved. Consider the blood transfusion needed to save that eight-year-old's life, though the parents' religious faith forbids blood transfusions. Either the child suffers harm (dies) and the parents suffer the loss of a child, or the parents' faith and values are harmed by performing the transfusion and saving the child's life against their deep religious beliefs. Typically the ethical decision a Western society court makes is that the child is not old enough to be able to make a lifelong commitment to a religious belief and therefore cannot make the choice to refuse the blood transfusion based on religious grounds. As well, the parents cannot be allowed to force a religious decision on the child, who may not commit to that religion. In a region where that religion is the predominant faith, what would a court decide?

IN PRACTICE

LET'S RETURN TO my opening story of maintenance workers taking the team training and being uncomfortable with having to sing and play musical instruments. Would you agree with the instructors that it was acceptable to make the workers uncomfortable as it was needed to help them learn? By unnecessarily making them uncomfortable and embarrassed, harm was done, and that is clearly unethical treatment. There is an implied social contract between instructors and students in that it is assumed the students will be treated fairly and with respect. I would argue that the instructors' actions were unethical as the workers knew they were not being treated with respect. This violates the implied social contract and, by extension, has a negative effect on the workers' learning and their attitude toward future training courses.

One time I was taking a two-day course, and after lunch on

the first day, the room felt very cold. I noticed other people were feeling cool as well. When we came to the first break, I searched for the thermostat to see at what temperature it was set. It was set at 18°C (65°F), which is cold if you're just sitting still. Just as I was turning up the temperature, the instructor came over, thanked me for turning it up, then told me what it had been set at earlier, and said she had turned it down after lunch. I asked why (we were putting the temperature back to where it was all morning, so obviously she hadn't turned it down because she was too warm). She told me that after people eat lunch they get sleepy and lethargic, so by turning the temperature down it would keep the students awake and more alert. That may be true, but it also makes the students unnecessarily uncomfortable for ninety minutes, and I know my focus on learning the material was distracted by the cool temperature. If the instructor had thought for a moment, *Is this a good idea? Will harm come to anyone?* she would have realized, *Yes, if I turn the temperature down that low, people will feel physically uncomfortable for an extended period of time, and in learning terms, any benefits of alertness will be offset by the distraction.* You might argue that sitting in a cool room isn't harmful. I would say harm has degrees or levels, and situations like this would fall at the very low end of the harm spectrum. The instructor would have been much better served by leaving the temperature alone and having the students participate in an active lesson immediately after lunch so they would not be sitting. Suffice it to say that the next day I and the others whom I told of the instructor's strategy brought heavy sweaters to wear after lunch.

CONCLUSION

THE BEST ADVICE I can give you is to consider the Hippocratic oath's mandate of "Do no harm." Furthermore, when you are confronted with only options where no decision will work for all (i.e., one or more people will suffer some form of harm), apply the principle of benefit maximization where you determine which decision leads to the greatest benefit or will benefit the most people. The final consideration is to reflect and make sure you are not fooling yourself (something I think we occasionally catch ourselves doing). By this I mean to consider if any of your decisions are putting you on a slippery slope. Ethical decisions can be very difficult, but I think that if you apply these three lines of thinking, you will make mostly good decisions. And for those that turn out to be bad, you'll know you gave the decision due consideration, which is all you can ask.

CHAPTER 12

Procedures and Work Instructions

INTRODUCTION

MOST OF MY experience with procedures has come from the chemical industry and the oil and gas industry. I do have some limited experience with written procedures from the medical industry and the aircraft industry as well. In all these industries, personal injury and death are potential consequences of human error. Procedures provide a barrier to these dire consequences; furthermore, they enable a best practice to be consistently repeated by all workers. This provides for safer and more effective and efficient work execution. In everyday life, adults are great at figuring out the fastest, easiest, most effective, cheapest way to learn whatever it is they're trying to figure out (Tough 1971). A well-thought-out, well-written, and properly designed procedure provides the adult user with exactly what he needs to aid him in performing certain tasks.

The first step is to determine if a procedure should even be written. The following is a short list of questions. If your answer is yes to any of these questions, then you should proceed with preparing a procedure. If your answer to all the questions is no, then a procedure is not required.

- Are there actions that can be easily overlooked?
- Is the task or equipment complex?
- Is the equipment critical?
- Are the tasks performed infrequently?
- Is there a regulatory requirement?

There should be an overriding document for creating and/or modifying procedures. In this document, other rules for when a procedure is required should be specified, for example, starting up or shutting a down equipment or a plant process if there is a safety risk.

My first experience with procedures was reading the repair manual I bought for my first car. It had step-by-step instructions for any repair, and I think I used most of those instructions for repairing that car. I could have never kept that car running without that manual. When I had a problem with the car, I would often take it to an automotive repair shop for a free diagnosis. They would tell me what was wrong, and I would buy the part(s), go home, and with the aid of the manual, successfully execute the needed repair. In thinking about that manual, I wonder what made it so good. As I recall, every repair went exactly according to the instructions provided, and it provided pictures and diagrams that were helpful.

An effective procedure is one that is clear and unambiguous and can be repeated with equal success by anyone with the prerequisite knowledge for performing the procedure (e.g., a registered nurse, a power engineer, a millwright). The following provides guidance to developing effective procedures.

Each procedure needs a title relevant to the purpose of the procedure. Each section included in the procedure needs to have a heading relevant to the content. Users will more quickly pick up and comprehend information when they have a brief preview of it.

There needs to be a balance in the style with lots of open space as this creates a user-friendly impression, compared to a procedure with a lot of pages or with pages completely filled with text, which becomes cumbersome and reduces the odds it will be used effectively.

Keep procedures as similar as possible in style and formatting. You want the users to feel comfortable and familiar. This is enabled by having procedures with the same look and feel, which creates a level of comfort. A style guide should be developed, and all procedures should follow the style and formatting rules laid out in the style guide.

Keep everything consistent since a consistent style and format lends itself to proper execution of the procedure. It's important that the users know what type of information will be provided and how it will be provided. This makes them not only comfortable with the procedure but also more confident. For the same reason, it's important that if something is spelled a certain way, or if capitals are used for certain things, it's done the same way every time. Consistent presentation demands the use of consistent terminology for naming components and equipment, a standard and effective format and page layout, and vocabulary suitable for the intended users.

With long procedures, there should be breaks along with

a summary to list what has transpired and a preview of what is about to occur. For example, a procedure might be broken up into segments like disassembly, measurement, and repair.

COMPONENTS OF A PROCEDURE

A PROCEDURE SHOULD include a few sections at the beginning. First, the procedure's purpose should be stated. The purpose conveys the procedure's goal, what it is that the procedure will enable the user to accomplish. Next you must articulate any prerequisites, initial conditions, or actions that need to be completed prior to commencing the procedure. The consequences of deviating or not using the procedure should be spelled out, for example, the potential for a serious health risk, a safety incident, or an environmental incident. If any safety gear needs to be worn at any point while performing the procedure's steps, the required safety gear needs to be clearly mentioned before the steps of the procedure are listed. Next, list in sequential order the step check and action descriptions that enable the user to carry out the procedure tasks. Depending on the procedure, appendices may be required at the end. Appendix examples include specification sheets and forms where information is recorded through the course of the procedure, for example, before and after measurements.

SYMBOLS AND ICONS

VISUAL AIDS, INCLUDING, pictures, diagrams, symbols, and icons, are valuable additions to a procedure (for example the Caution icon on the following page). For electronic procedures accessed through mobile devices in the field, consider the use of short videos. The objective of the procedure is to help the user perform an activity in a precise and safe manner, so anything the writer can do to enable this is worth doing. Following this paragraph are common symbols that are important to use where appropriate. As a cost-cutting measure, many companies prefer that documents not be printed in color. However, where possible, procedures should be printed in color. Thankfully as we move more and more toward an online connected world, this will not be an issue, as procedure use will be performed using a handheld electronic device. By using color, more attention is drawn to the symbols, which helps to convey important information. Because of publishing restraints I have had to keep the examples in *The Handbook for Learning and Development Professionals* in black and white.

Caution symbols are typically only used to alert users to actions or conditions that could result in equipment damage, environmental releases, or major quality problems.

Danger symbols are typically only used to alert users to actions or conditions that could result in injury or death.
Both caution and danger symbols need to appear at the step that presents the concern.

NOTICE

Notice symbols are typically used to help the user perform the step. The notice symbol alerts the user to the unexpected and provides other needed information that a user may not know. Notice symbols should not contain "nice to know" information.

Pencil symbols appear where there are instructions to record data, for example, measurements on the specification sheet.
Caution, danger, notice, and pencil symbols need to appear at the step to which they apply. Place the symbol and associated information directly at the step and action that the symbol relates to. I've seen lists at the beginning of a procedure, and while this works, it is not nearly as effective.

STYLE AND FORMAT

SERIF FONTS ARE easiest to read. This style of font was designed after extensive research to develop a font that is easy for readers to read. Making the font easy to read enables the reader to read more quickly with less strain and to comprehend the material better. Most magazines use this style of font for these exact reasons. For hard-copy procedures, 12 point font is a good size as it is large enough to easily read under most lighting conditions. Font size can be tested with the users to see what size works best for them.

IT IS MORE DIFFICULT TO READ WHEN THE TEXT IS DISPLAYED IN ALL CAPITAL LETTERS. Furthermore, this has the negative connation that writer is yelling. For these reasons, avoid any temptation to write a procedure in all capital letters. I've seen too many procedures written using all capital letters. This is not to say that certain words cannot be in all capitals as it can work to use all capitals for the main verb in a step action (e.g., CLOSE upstream block valve to the high-pressure brine pump). Another effective technique for placing greater emphasis on certain words is to boldface the keywords.

PAGE FORMAT AND LAYOUT OF A PROCEDURE

OPEN PAGE FORMATTING is a style where the page has a large amount of open space; this style is less intimidating for the user, versus a page packed with text. A user's first glance at a page that is all text tends to result in a blur of gray and makes following the procedure more difficult, especially in field conditions. Consider the use of pictures and diagrams, anything that can help the end user to better understand how to execute the procedure.

There are two common types of procedure formats:

1. **T format** divides the page into two columns, which can vary in width depending on the type and amount of information you need to enter. This style can be set up to leave plenty of open space on the page and create a pleasant functional procedure.

2. **Table format** uses a table-style layout. The horizontal lines of the table aid the user in reading and following the procedure. Care needs to be taken to ensure ample open space is used.

The following is a very basic example of a T-format style for a procedure:

Step	Action	Notes
1 ☐	Jack up front of car using floor jack.	Approximately 16" behind the front edge of the center of the car, there is a marked lifting pad for the jack.
2 ☐	Place jack stands under the frame on each side of the car behind the front tires.	**DANGER** Do not under any circumstances place any part of your body under the car without the protection of the jack stands.
3 ☐	Lower the car onto the jack stands, allowing the jack stands to support the car's weight.	
4 ☐	Place wheel chocks behind rear tires.	
5 ☐	Place oil catch pan under the car's oil pan.	**CAUTION** Ensure the oil catch pan is located so that all the oil drains into the pan.
6 ☐	Remove drain plug, and allow time for oil to fully drain.	Removal of the drain plug requires a 9/16" socket or wrench.
7 ☐	Once the oil is fully drained, replace the drain plug.	Torque the drain plug to 40 ft-lb.
8 ☐	Place the drain pan under the oil filter.	

9 ☐	Remove oil filter, place right side up in drain pan, and allow time for oil to drain.	✏	While waiting for oil to drain, record car's mileage on maintenance M-17 form.

The following is a very basic example of a table-format style for a procedure:

Step	Initial	Action
1		Jack up front of car using floor jack.
	NOTICE	*Approximately 16" behind the front bumper in the center of the car, there is a marked lifting pad for the jack.*
2		Place jack stands under the frame on each side of the car behind the front tires.
	DANGER	*Do not under any circumstances place any part of your body under the car without the protection of the jack stands.*
3		Lower the car onto the jack stands, allowing the jack stands to support the car's weight.
4		Place wheel chocks behind rear tires.
5		Place oil catch pan under the car's oil pan.
	CAUTION	*Ensure the oil catch pan is located so that all the oil drains into the pan.*
6		Remove drain plug, and allow time for oil to fully drain.
	NOTICE	*Removal of the drain plug requires a 9/16" socket or wrench.*

7		Once the oil is fully drained, replace the drain plug.
	NOTICE	*Torque the drain plug to 40 ft-lb.*
8		Place the drain pan under the oil filter.
9		Remove oil filter and place right side up in drain pan. Allow time for oil to drain.
		While waiting for oil to drain, record car's mileage on maintenance M-17 form.

THE THEORETICAL SIDE OF WRITING A PROCEDURE

IT IS EASIER to read and understand shorter lines of text. Once you've written the initial draft for a procedure, review it and edit the writing. Keep the sentences as short and to the point as possible.

On average, people will process and remember about five to seven units of information at one time. As writers we need to ensure we never present more than five pieces/units of information at a time. If you need to list some items in a procedure, do not have a list of more than five items. You may need to break the instructions up and present two or more lists to do this.

Procedures need to be as consistent as possible in terms of wording, style, fonts, icons, warnings, cautions, and notes. This type of consistency enables the reader to process the information more quickly. Creative writing, like what we are taught in school, teaches us to write in a manner that keeps the reader's interest, therefore this type of consistency would mean repetitiveness and go against keeping the reader's interest. However, in procedure writing the purpose is to transfer information, not to entertain. A repetitive style enables the reader to find things quickly, or allows the reader spot what can be skipped quickly, making it much more efficient at knowledge transfer.

All of the information in the procedure should be directly relevant to the purpose of the procedure. Irrelevant or "nice to know" information needs to be separated or left out completely. When irrelevant information is included, it not only takes time for the reader to read it, but then the reader invariably tries to figure out how it belongs. All this wastes time and leads to confusion and less comprehension on the user's part.

Each procedure needs a title relevant to the purpose of the procedure. Each section included in the procedure needs to have a heading relevant to the content of that section. Besides being good practice, the procedure's users will more quickly pick up and comprehend information when they have a brief preview to it.

THE PRACTICAL SIDE OF WRITING A PROCEDURE

WHEN WRITING A procedure, the first and foremost thing to do is to write the procedure's goal (purpose) to ensure that once the procedure is completed, it accomplishes the goal.

Examine the amount of information you've included. If you provide too little information, the novice won't use the procedure. If you provide too much detail, experienced workers will view it as hard to follow, and therefore they won't use the procedure either. You need to consider the intended users' level of responsibility, training, experience, and capability. There's no magic formula— you just need to consider the foregoing, do your best, get one of the intended users to give you some feedback, and then make any adjustments at that point.

Brief steps and consistent format lend themselves to proper use of the document.

Completeness is not a function of the procedure's length or detail; it's a function of whether or not it has enough information for users to perform the task safely and correctly.

Review the completed procedure and eliminate detail and language that does not contribute to work performance, safety, or quality. The procedure needs to contain only "need to know" information and not any "nice to know" information. For example, a power engineer needs to know how to use a flammable gas detector and where to use it, whereas it is merely nice to know how it works.

Always identify cautions, warnings, and notes in the same way. A note should contain only explanatory information to allow the user to avoid the unexpected and perform the task safely. It should not contain actions or "nice to knows." Do not get in the habit of writing lots of notes, cautions, and warnings, as this can lead to unintentionally hiding the steps/actions from the users. It can also desensitize the user to the notes, cautions, and warnings.

Keep the procedure steps as simple as possible with a maximum of two related actions for each step (e.g., CLOSE and LOCK valve).

Try to avoid using the following types of procedure steps:

- Go to step 7.
- Return to step 4.
- Refer to step 9.

It is not good practice to have the user skipping around to find things. These types of steps are a recipe for the procedure not to be completed properly. In some cases, these types of steps cannot be avoided, but analyze anytime you need to use a step like this and ensure it is the best way, not just the easiest way, for you to write the procedure.

If the information in a procedure cannot be used or understood, it is useless. A procedure can be technically correct but be totally ineffective for this reason. Having an intended user use the procedure as a trial or pilot can be invaluable.

Following are some questions to ask about the procedure you've just written:

1. Can the actions be performed as written in the sequence given?
2. Does the user have the training/knowledge needed to carry out the procedure?
3. Does the user need to be alerted to any potential hazards or require any supporting information?
4. Does the user need to know any specifics not mentioned in the procedure?
5. Is needed information found someplace else (e.g., on a graph, panel display, or chart)?
6. Are the steps in logical order?
7. What are the results of improper task performance? (If an action is critical, spell it out.)

CONCLUSION

PROCEDURES CAN BE valuable work aids. It is important to maintain a consistent look and feel not only within each procedure but also across all your procedures. Well-written procedures can become integral to your overall training program. Your program should have an overarching document that outlines the use of formatting, style, icon usage, titling, and headings to ensure the procedures are written with a purpose and achieve their stated purpose.

CHAPTER 13

Program Planning

INTRODUCTION

PROGRAM PLANNING IS best described as an analysis process that is utilized to develop a learning program, which is defined as everything from course development to course and program evaluation, through to marketing of the program and its offerings. Once established, a program plan contributes to future development within the program by guiding changes using the process elements initially created in developing the program. Having a program plan ensures efficiency and effectiveness. Creating a program or its elements without a defined program planning process will result, at best, in a patchwork quilt of best practices. A well-thought-out program planning process prevents overlapping work and lacunae. The end goal is to have a strategic, integrated, fit-for-purpose program.

In this chapter, the basics of program planning and a generic process are described. Each situation is different, but the content of this chapter will provide a learning and development professional with the knowledge needed to develop a program planning process for his or her unique environment. Every learning and development team should have a documented program planning process. *Program Planning for Adult Learners*, written by Rosemary Caffarella, is a very good book on subject. My copy of this text comes from 1994, in which the book's foreword was written by Malcolm Knowles; it is high praise to have the full endorsement of one of the masters!

PROGRAM PLANNING PROCESS OVERVIEW

ALL PROGRAMS SHOULD be learner-focused so that everything is built with the learner in mind. There are lots of other factors that need to be considered. First, the context the program exists within needs to be considered. The internal and external factors need to be understood. Internal factors range from organizational dynamics, budgets, resources, and staffing to stakeholders, history, and values. External factors include the learning and development team's support from management, relationships with other departments, and whether these relationships are competitive or collaborative. How would or how is the learning and development program perceived by the end users? In general, what is the cultural, economic, and political climate for learning and development in the company?

The elements that support the learner and the overall program are discussed in greater detail in the other chapters of *The Handbook for the Learning and Development Professional.* The key is to have all the elements aligned and supporting one another. The following list and descriptions cover the elements of making a comprehensive program plan:

VISION AND MISSION

A MISSION STATEMENT is used to describe the learning and development team's function and how it contributes to the bigger organization. A simple example would be: "Our learning, development, and competency assurance program ensures our company's workers are competent to safely and effectively perform their jobs."

A vision statement should state the learning and development team's vision of what success is now and in the future. Here's a simple example of a vision statement: "Our talent development and competency assurance program will meet or exceed all regulatory requirements in the areas of health, safety, the environment, and technical competency."

You can choose to have both a mission and vision statement or some other form of overriding directional statement. It is important to develop a high-level statement (or two in combination) that your company president would agree with. This sets the stage for the elements of your program plan, starting with its objectives.

Objectives. What are the program's objectives? Objectives vary and might include delivering safety knowledge, technical capacity growth, skill improvement, and soft skill development. Knowing what the main overriding objectives of the program plan are drives the proper decisions on all aspects of the program plan. These objectives need to be stated and agreed upon early in the process. The individual courses and directed learning deliver on the objectives.

Needs analysis. This was discussed in detail in chapter 6. In summary, a formal, repeatable process needs to be decided on. The needs of the learners drive the other decisions made about the program plan. What is it exactly that the workers need to learn, develop, and/or improve on?

Resources. Obviously there's no point building a program that will not have the resources it requires to be executed. Understanding the resources the learning and development team has to work with is key to building the program. This starts with what the staffing level will be in the learning and development group and moves on to include office space, training rooms, IT support, and budget amounts. What will you have to work with, and what are the limitations?

Budget. As mentioned, knowing the budget is vital to building a program plan. You wouldn't build a house without knowing how much money it will cost and without knowing what your yearly income is projected to be. Budget will be dictated, or will you need to build a case? Based on a projected needs analysis, list out what is needed, the options for delivering what is needed, and how much each item costs. Specify the period of time in which the program will take place and what the priorities are from among all the needs.

Implementation. A timeline or project plan needs to be developed detailing when each step of the entire plan will be completed and how long it will take. This will enable you to know when various items need to be rolled out to managers and/or the workers. This needs to be developed in conjunction with a communication plan.

Communication. Details about what needs to be communicated should be determined and written out. In examining what needs to be communicated, you should, for each item, determine who needs to receive this communication. Next you will need to determine the best method(s) for communicating each of these items. Should the method used vary for different receiving groups? Sending emails is all too easy in today's world. The problem innocently becomes this: what's being rolled out doesn't seem like a difficult thing to those rolling it out. They fail to realize they've been working on the project for months, so to them it is now simple. As a result of their comfort and familiarity with the topic, they roll out the project to those who now must execute the work. The problem is that they do this without fully appreciating those people's unfamiliarity and comfort level with what is being rolled out.

For example, there's a new process for entering personal expenses. The people on the receiving end may not even read the email carefully, if at all, because they get so many. It may seem straightforward to those who were working on it and developing it for the last few months, but it may be difficult for those receiving the email to figure it out. Today many emails no longer seem all that important, so important ones can get lost in the maze. As a result, you might have people with varying levels of understanding and the feeling of no support. Now you have a frustrated group of people. Some things are small enough and simple enough that an email is an acceptable method of communication, whereas other things require face-to-face meetings. You need a strategy for dealing with various information and projects that will be rolled out, because the success of what is rolled out depends a great deal on the quality of the way it is communicated to the end users.

Ongoing communication is another important detail. What needs to be communicated regularly? How often, and to whom? Training compliance reports are an obvious example. These typically go out to managers and supervisors monthly. What about training schedules, upcoming courses, and so on? What is the best method in your company for communicating these items?

Marketing. This can be a part of your communication

plan/strategy. Often in a company's learning and development department, the marketing element gets overlooked because they have a captive audience. It is important to sell the benefits of the program and of individual courses, showing how they benefit individuals and the company as a whole. In many companies, soft skills training is optional. Good marketing of these courses can be valuable in getting people to sign up. If people do sign up and attend, they will gain knowledge and skills that enable the company to be more productive. It's a win-win that the training group owns.

Evaluations. Chapter 11 covered the details of course and program evaluation. In the program planning, how this will happen needs to be articulated. What evaluations will occur and when? What will be the focus? A postcourse survey (level 1) should be designed as part of the program plan. Will different courses or different types of courses require a different level 1 survey? Details with respect to what other levels will be applied and how they will be applied should be spelled out in the program plan, as should a description of how the results from the evaluations will be applied back to the program for improvement. At what intervals will the evaluation data be examined? The results from a single level 1 survey can be helpful, but the combined results from five hundred surveys provide more in-depth data and trends. It needs to be determined what actions one survey result can drive and after how many a composite examination will take place. How will the level 1 results be conflated with the findings of levels 2 and 3? These should all be determined in advance of executing the evaluations.

Reassessment. The program plan should identify criteria for reassessing the plan. This could be time-driven, for example, every other year. Or it could be driven by other criteria, such as budget cuts. When the price of oil dropped dramatically in the mid-2010s, oil and gas companies cut all their departments' budgets, and a great number of people had to be laid off for the businesses to survive. When my learning and development budget and resources were cut significantly, one of the first things I did was to meet with my team and revisit the program plan; it had to change to reflect the new operating environment.

Environment. What positive and negative influences exist in your company with respect to executing a learning and development strategy? To what degree does senior management support learning and development, and to what degree in which areas? An industrial company may strongly support safety training but at the same time have low support for technical training. A retail-based company may support sales training more than safety training. This knowledge will drive decisions regarding what type of training will be supported for delivery. It also defines what conversations need to take place if the needs analysis shows other types of training are required, particularly if management does not support such training. Understanding the environment in which the program is being executed drives better, quicker decisions.

CONCLUSION

DEVELOPING A WRITTEN program plan starting with an overriding statement (or a combination of two statements) along with supporting objectives is necessary to ensure your learning and development output is a strategic, integrated program that is fit for purpose. A program plan ensures the program can be reassessed and continually improved. It ensures that the learning and development program delivered to the company fully utilizes all the resources afforded it and that there are no gaps in what it needs to deliver. Developing a solid program plan involves participation from the many stakeholders in the organization, which aids in the program's buy-in and success.

CHAPTER 14

Learning Management Systems

A LEARNING MANAGEMENT system (LMS) can be all-encompassing like SAP SuccessFactors (which contains all student information, courses, assessments, records, scheduling, rooms, and calendars—and more). There are some smaller or more specialized LMS's that tend to be more learning focused and less HR focused. Some contain and deliver learning content. These are known as learning content management systems (LCMS). To be perfectly honest, I haven't seen an LMS that I like, but at the same time I couldn't run an L & D department without one. The bigger ones that combine LMS and LCMS seem to try to do too much from one point, and because of this they become too complex. It's kind of like if you were to combine all of Microsoft's programs into one program with everything originating from one window. However,

LMS's are hard to live without as they are very good for holding and managing all things related to learning. Each LMS comes with its own four-inch (or more) binder manual, so I'm not going to get into the operating of the LMS here. I do have a few points for those moving to or transitioning to a new LMS. Hopefully you haven't learned these lessons the way I have, that is, the hard way.

If you are about to transition to a LMS/LCMS, my strong advice is this: do not underestimate how complex these programs are. Set everything up with strict naming conventions; all your courses, curriculums, training rooms, and so on should be titled for quick and easy identification. I've worked for multinational companies where prefixes were not given to courses to identify them, resulting in dozens of versions of a course for the different locations around the world. It was a nightmare for anyone trying to figure out which one was for their geographic location. When the old LMS became outdated and was no longer supported, we had to transition to a new one, and this unorganized mess made the job exponentially more difficult and expensive. We found courses with identical content but with slightly different naming conventions among different departments at the same location. It was messy to sort out. Life with an LMS is so much easier if everything is very well organized.

Look at the LMS as a big library.

The following is an example of a course naming convention:

NAB.CDN.MTCE.MW-Centrifical_Compressor_Overhaul

NAB indicates the location: Northern Alberta. CDN indicates the country: Canada. MTCE indicates the department: maintenance. MW indicates who in maintenance the training is for: millwrights. Centrifugal_Compressor_Overhaul indicates the course name.

What can happen is that the course initially is set up as just Centrifugal Compressor Overhaul. Then another location enters a course for the same procedure, but since the name is already taken, they name it Overhaul Centrifugal Compressors. And then another location will name it differently, and so on. Then a user (or a new learning admin staffer who's trying to sign people up for courses) goes looking for the course only to find nine, and they have no idea which one they should choose. So, again, what should be a simple action becomes an exercise in frustration. Following naming conventions similar to the example shown will save you a great deal of frustration down the road.

LMS's display search results alphabetically. Carefully consider everything you enter into an LMS; know what can be changed and what will stay in the system forever. I cannot stress this enough: careful planning in the beginning will pay many dividends later.

Given how complex an LMS is and can become, I recommend limiting the number of people who have full access. It is best to have just a few people who work with the LMS on a daily basis. It is much more efficient this way. Given my position over the years, I'm one of those people who once a week has to go into the LMS, but seldom for the same thing as last week or the week before. I inevitably find myself looking for my cheat notes on how to do what it is I'm attempting to do. Dedicated people who use the LMS daily typically use the features frequently enough and have used them often enough to have most things memorized.

If you are moving to an LMS for the first time or are transitioning, do not underestimate how much work it involves. I strongly recommend having a project manager and a dedicated team. Allocate the time of the L & D staff for the project. I've seen it both ways, and with the proper manpower and planning, the transition happens quickly and reasonably smoothly. Trying to just have the L & D staff do it while keeping up with their current duties stretches the implementation out over a longer time and creates frustration on the L & D staff side and, more importantly, on the end user side as well. The expression in the real estate business is that the three most important things are location, location, location. I would counter that by saying the three most important elements with an LMS are be organized, be organized, be organized!

CHAPTER 15

Leadership

INTRODUCTION

TOO OFTEN IN today's workplace I see people who become the early adopters of a new company directive being described as leaders for doing so. In many workplace situations, leadership has come to mean "early follower." The meaning of leadership is getting lost as too many managers use the term to coerce their workers into being followers, with the reward being "I'll recognize you as a leader"—and leadership is what leads to promotions.

What exactly is leadership? In this chapter I'll briefly outline several of the more common and practical theories on leadership and briefly discuss postmodernism's influence. It's up to the individual to determine what style fits you for a given situation. Suffice it to say, though, that to lead isn't to follow, even if you're the first follower. Leadership is gaining the support of others to pursue a worthwhile objective.

TRANSFORMATIONAL LEADERSHIP THEORY

TRANSFORMATIONAL LEADERS CAN be found at any and all levels in an organization. They are visionary, motivating, and risk-taking thinkers. While they may exhibit charisma, more importantly they have four main attributes:

1. **Inspirational motivation.** This is achieved through the presentation of a vision, a mission, and a set of values. The vision has deep meaning for, and is found to be challenging by, the followers. This creates an environment of camaraderie and commitment to achieving the vision.

2. **Intellectual stimulation.** Transformational leaders encourage creativity and innovation in their followers. They create an atmosphere that nurtures creativity and innovation and allows for the challenging and discarding of old ways or methods, not blaming or criticizing members in the process. They keep the focus of problems on the what, not on the who.

3. **Idealized influence.** Such leaders hold and live to a high ethical standard. As the leaders, they deeply believe that the best way to influence their followers is to lead by example, so they walk their talk. Through this approach they gain respect and trust. They put their followers' needs above their own. They use their power to get everyone to work toward the organization's goals.

4. **Individualized consideration.** When the members display the behavior desired, for example, creativity and

innovation, the transformational leader rewards them. Members in this type of leadership scenario are empowered to make decisions, and the leader ensures the support is there for them to follow through with those decisions. The members are treated individually based on their knowledge and skills.

The following are examples of potential weaknesses of the transformational leadership theory:

- It can lead to self-promotion by its proponents as a result of its use of impression management.
- This style is really the combination of many styles coming together in various ways, so this makes it very hard to train people in using and applying this leadership theory.
- There's potential for the followers to be led astray by leaders who become manipulative.

The current environment characterized by uncertainty, global turbulence, and organizational instability calls for transformational leadership to prevail at all levels of the organization. The followers of such leaders demonstrate high levels of job satisfaction and organizational commitment and engage in organizational citizenship behaviors. With such a devoted workforce, it is definitely useful to transform the organization through leadership (Management Study Guide.com 2011).

Transformational leadership can be grandiose in nature, resulting in large-scale, large-impact change, though there may be small-scale change too. It's a leadership style, so like with all the others, the magnitude of the vision does not make this style more or less applicable.

TRAIT LEADERSHIP THEORY

THIS THEORY IS based on the assumption that leadership requires certain characteristics or traits. The idea is that leaders have all these traits, and new leaders can be found by either identifying people with these traits or developing these traits in others. Stogdill (1974) identified a series of skills and traits he determined to be essential for a leader to have. The skills were above-average intelligence; conceptually skill; creativity; diplomacy and tactfulness; fluent speaking; knowledge of the group's task(s); and being well organized, persuasive, and socially adept. The traits Stogdill identified were adaptability to situations; assertiveness; decisiveness; cooperation; attentiveness to the social environment; the desire to influence others; ambitiousness; and being achievement-oriented, self-confident, dependable, willing to assume responsibility, tolerant of stress, and high in energy level.

Practical limitations of this theory include the fact that determining who is a good leader and to what degree such people are good leaders is a very subjective exercise. The next problem comes in determining if certain traits are more important than others, and if so, what the ranking order is and how much weight is given to each trait. In considering this, it's important to note that over one hundred traits of successful leaders have been identified.

EMERGENT LEADERSHIP THEORY

THE BASIC IDEA of this leadership theory is that in any given situation, leaders will arise from the group. With the proper dynamics, the person or people best suited to lead a particular circumstance, based on their knowledge, experience, and skills, will be the ones who take the lead. A study by Tuckman (1965) looked at how groups evolve. The study revealed that there are four distinctive steps in the process. Step 1 is the testing and dependence between the group members, with step 2 being conflict among group members. At step 3, cohesion develops among and throughout the group, and by step 4, functional maturity increases with time and challenges. Out of this theory came the idea that emergent leaders develop from initially being oriented to the group, then once in the group working through conflicts, finally to emerge as the leader. The conflicts and challenges that the group faces enable the potential leader to establish his or her credibility with the group and gain their confidence. This results in the leader's being able to exercise his or her influence.

CONTINGENCY THEORY AND LEADERSHIP

THE IDEA BEHIND this theory is that every situation is different, so what works as effective leadership in one situation may not work in another. Some people will excel as leaders in one situation but fail in others. This explains why sometimes we see people doing an excellent job of leadership only to fail later; this theory would suggest that such occurrences are the result of the situation slowly changing to the point where that person's style is no longer effective. Situational leadership theory is similar, though this theory suggests that the leader change his or her approach to match the particular known situation. Contingency leadership, on the other hand, assumes the leader has one style and that the style, to be effective, must suit a given situation (Value Based Management.net 2016).

COMPLEXITY LEADERSHIP THEORY

THIS CONCEPT DESCRIBES three types of leadership present in organizations, namely, adaptive, administrative, and enabling. Numerous research papers have been written on this theory from a mathematical and computational perspective.

Hazy (2008) suggests that human dynamics in a system made up of people in a social network can be studied by using computational modeling to determine what leadership might look like in that complex adaptive system. Hazy states that in looking at leadership this way, there are five actions that need to be taken:

1. Identify or espouse a cooperation strategy or program.
2. Catalyze conditions where other agents choose to participate in the program.
3. Organize choices and actions in other agents to navigate complexity and avoid interaction catastrophe (sometimes called "complexity catastrophe").
4. Form a distinct output layer that expresses the system as a unity in its environment.
5. Translate feedback into structural changes in the network of influence among agents.

Research on this theory has looked at how leadership affects success and failure. The theory takes the position that leadership does not come from solely one individual but comes from many people within the organization. The idea is that you must not only observe what each of these individuals contribute but also determine what access they have to organizational capabilities. This system (organization) adapts to any tension that is placed on it.

TRANSACTIONAL LEADERSHIP THEORY

THIS THEORY WORKS on the notion that people are motivated by rewards and punishment. The follower is typically a subordinate who accepts that the leader has full authority to direct the former as the latter feels necessary, and the job of the former is to execute those directions. This type of leadership tends to exist in situations where there is a clear hierarchy and chain of command. The leader supports and maintains a clearly defined structure and ensures that what is expected of the followers is clearly expressed. A good example is a company where a person is hired and given pay and benefits; she is told where she fits in the company structure, whom she reports to, and by extension whose orders she follows. The company then has rewards for high performers and punishments in place for insubordination.

A limitation of this theory is that it assumes people are simple enough to have predictable behaviors based solely on the idea of reward and punishment in exchange for following directions (Management Study Guide.com 2011).

DISTRIBUTED LEADERSHIP THEORY

DISTRIBUTED LEADERSHIP IS often referred to as shared leadership, democratic leadership, or team leadership. This method of leadership allows for leadership to be executed from all levels of an organization, not just from the traditional roles of power and authority. The ability of people at all levels of an organization to have influence is seen as essential, and this influence derived from everyone helps to set the direction. It is a method that is about leadership practice, as all the people in an organization share the leadership. Leadership is not about the traits and skills of one or a few individuals in positions of authority; rather, distributed leadership sees leadership as a group quality. It is seen as a method that can produce at a level greater than the sum of its parts, whereas other, more traditional styles of leadership that rely on leaders in positions of power and authority cannot produce in such a way. It is important to note that this method does not eliminate those leaders who are in positions of power and authority, but it is a method that leverages leadership from others beyond just the people in such positions (Harris 2008).

According to Bolden (2011), distributed leadership theory is based on three concepts:

1. Leadership is a property that arises out of a group (network) of people.
2. The boundaries of leadership are open and not confined in traditional ways.
3. The diversity of expertise within the group is shared.

This means that leadership coming out of the group is really leadership developed from a social network, and as such it is culturally sensitive. These networks will have to arrive at common understandings. The strength in this theory is that in practice, the organization should have the right people with the right expertise for any given situation be the ones who take the lead. In essence an organization should have fluidity of leaders and styles based on the needs and circumstances.

CONCLUSION

IN ANY ORGANIZATION there is a need for leadership; it may be to run the organization to maintain the status quo, to lead the organization to capture growth opportunities, or to lead the organization through necessary change to survive. The rate of change and improvement in technology has outpaced that of social attitudes and political establishments, so these advancements have the potential to be leveraged for the greater benefit of society. The same applies to the fields of education, learning, and development, where organizational transformation needs to be achieved in order to improve the product and keep pace with the advancements in science and technology (Latchem and Hanna 2001).

Postmodernism and the Future of Education

I PRESENT THIS for thought and reflection on where formal education and, by extension, corporate learning is going. Just what does the future hold? There's so much knowledge and change today that it can be hard to make sense and see the big picture, if it can be seen with any clarity to begin with.

Realism is about the dyad of truth and accuracy. In the arts this means portraying things as they are in reality from the artist's perception. The artist adds no emotional or romantic interpretations into his or her work. If something is an ugly truth, then it is portrayed that way. The Enlightenment's values coexist nicely with those of realism. The Enlightenment put forth a belief in science with rationality at its roots and a belief in being critical when thinking of accepted customs, institutions, and morals as these are what guide the world. Modernism is the belief that in the new modern industrialized world, the concepts of realism and enlightenment that support the traditional forms of art, literature, religion, and social institutions are outdated and ineffective.

> Modernism requires faith that there are universals that can be discovered through reason, that science and the scientific method are superior means for arriving at truth and reality, and that language describes and can be used as a credible and reliable

means of access to that reality. With its privileging of reason, modernism has long been considered the basis for the emancipation of men and women from the bonds of ignorance associated with stagnant tradition, narrow religions, and meager educations. Championing democracy, modernism promises freedom, equality, justice, the good life, and prosperity. Equating merit with high culture, modernism provides expectations of more rigorous standards for and greater enjoyment of the arts and architecture. Through science and scientific method, modernism promises health, the eradication of hunger, crime, and poverty. Modernist science claims to be progressing toward true knowledge of the universe and to be delivering ever higher standards of living with effectiveness and efficiency. Modernism promises stability, peace, and a graspable sense of the rational unfolding of history. Modernism equates change with progress, which is defined as increasing control over nature and society. The concept of Modernism is that humans have the power to create, change, and improve their environment with the help of science and technology. (Bloland 1995, 523)

Postmodernism assails modernist values and its institutions and sees modernism as destructive, inadequate, and costly. Postsecondary institutions are seen as pillars of modernism. As a result, any attack on modernism is an attack on the system of higher education. Postmodernist Derrida (1976) describes the hierarchies that exist in higher education. He then suggests that the hierarchies (existing in higher education) create a delegitimation that results in these institutions being unable to see true reality. Foucault's (1979) archaeological approach focuses on the power and knowledge relationships that exist in institutions for higher learning. The idea is that the two have to coexist, and therefore the knowledge that arises from research always has power implications. As a result, no knowledge can ever be truly neutral or completely objective. The questions in institutions of higher learning become, who has the power, how do they wield it, and what are the effects of that? Metanarratives are the universal beliefs that underpin our orientation to the world. Lyotard (1984) questions the influence of these metanarratives. The foundations of institutions of higher education are based upon these metanarratives, such as the assumptions around knowledge, progress, socialization, and science.

Postmodernist Baudrillard (1983) proposes the term implosion, where the boundary between simulation and reality is erased and implodes. Universities are losing their monopoly on certain knowledge. If their hierarchies begin to dissolve as Derrida suggests will happen, and if the metanarratives change, then the boundaries will move and/or disappear (Bloland 1995), or to use Baudrillard's (1983) terminology, the boundaries will implode. There are activities indicating that this process might have started; in recent years noticeable changes in institutions of higher education have appeared, for example, massive open online courses (MOOCs), in which some major universities are offering their best courses to anyone for free. Thousands may have signed up for such a course and contributed to the high participation numbers versus the low completion rates (less than 10 percent, according to Duke University 2013). One can surmise that these courses are attended not so much for university credit but apparently for the sake of learning something of interest within the course. This would seem to be at odds with modernism thinking in that higher education credentials lead to merit of some kind, which in turn leads to higher standing in the community and/or the working world (Bloland 1995). Online open universities in and of themselves are changing the traditional higher education hierarchies by opening enrollment up so widely to so many, and in locations where in the past university access was not possible. Are these events occurring as a result of postmodern thinking and influence, or are they merely extensions and adaptations resulting from modernism?

Postmodernism has impacted and changed our society's cultures, polity, and economy (Bloland 1995). Based on this observation, one can conclude postmodernism has and will continue to have an influence on open and higher education, as well as on corporate learning organizations. To what degree this will happen, which direction this will take, and where it will lead is not clear. We do know strong visionary leadership will be the elixir to cause postmodernism's influence to become the most beneficial for open education, higher education, and the corporate world of learning and development.

Summary: There are many theories on leadership—the trick is to apply the right one for a given situation, based on the person leading. The Learning and Development field varies greatly from being in a mostly static situation of delivering content to creating an entire program from the ground up—and everything in between. It offers everyone in the field opportunities for taking on formal and informal leadership roles. Success in these leadership roles will be greatly influenced by a person's ability to be an effective leader as well as by his or her technical expertise.

CHAPTER 16

Project Management

INTRODUCTION

PROJECT MANAGEMENT IS a disciplined approach to planning and executing a defined outcome, for example, bringing a learning management system (LMS) into an organization and having it replace many of the systems and methods currently being used. Projects need to have a defined scope. Part of the discipline is to stay within that defined scope. It is very easy to get into a project and think of other items that should be included (scope creep); once that's allowed to happen, the budget the project started with will run over, and the timeline that was agreed to when the project started will no longer be met. Careful thought, with as much input as is practical, is vital to properly define scope and thereby allow for the project's ultimate success.

The project manager will need to use a project plan. It needs to break down all the tasks that will need to be executed. These tasks need to be put on a timeline. This necessitates determining which tasks are dependent on others and in what order they need to be executed. It is important that a schedule be created for a project. This is typically done by using a Gantt chart. The project is either forward- or reverse-scheduled. Each task needs to be defined in terms of what activity or activities need to be executed. Then the activity's start date and completion date both need to be determined. Once the activity and its corresponding timeline details are known, it can be placed in the correct sequence on the Gantt chart. The sequencing will determine which task(s) can start when other tasks are completed. For all the tasks there is typically a critical path; this revolves around one aspect of the project where the series of tasks takes the longest to complete, and any delay in any of the critical path tasks will delay the completion of the project as a whole. Along with tracking the timeline, the costs need to be determined and tracked throughout the project. Depending on the size of the project, cost and time milestones that are achieved should be celebrated. Being highly organized and staying organized is important to completing a project successfully.

LEADERSHIP AND PROJECT MANAGEMENT

SUMNER, BOCK, AND Giamartino (2006) researched the success of IT projects in relation to a project manager's technical skills and leadership ability. The project managers were evaluated using a leadership practice inventory (LPI), a tool that measures leadership competencies by way of self-assessment and observer assessment. The LPI uses thirty questions, broken down into six questions each in five areas of leadership. No significant results were found in comparing the self-assessments to IT project success. However, with the observer LPI, all five categories were found to be statistically significant predictors of project success. This indicates that project leadership skills are equally important to success as are the project manager's technical skills of project scope management, project time management, project cost management, and project quality management (Sumner, Bock, and Giamartino 2006). I find this interesting as my experience in industry suggests that project managers are typically chosen for their project management skills with little thought given to their leadership skills. Project managers need to be aware that aside from the technical aspects of project planning, they must be equally focused on the leadership skill areas of interpersonal relationships, communications, cooperation, and collaboration.

PROJECT TEAM MEMBERS

ALLY, CLEVELAND-INNES, AND Wiseman examined project management in a teleworking situation. They defined this type of complex project as "a distance education project involving interconnected actors and institutions divided across spatial and temporal boundaries, working toward a unique product, service or result" (Ally, Cleveland-Innes, and Wiseman 2010, 1). Telework is described as the typical work activities that are carried out by project team members who work together and communicate from a distance using technology, ranging from telephones to computer networks using advanced software. The authors identified three main factors dealing with team members in order to complete a project successfully:

Selecting team members. The group must be organized in such a way that regular communication occurs among all members regardless of their position or location. It is important to select team members who will be committed and willing to contribute to the team and project. This can be achieved by selecting members whom the organization has trust in and feels a positive relationship with. Maintaining commitment can be a challenge, so the project manager's leadership skills, managerial skills, and ability to listen to the team is essential.

Orientating team members. It needs to be made clear what each member's responsibilities are. Planning and structure are vital, especially if the workers have autonomy and will be working with little supervision. It is important to have a known schedule broken into sections for everyone to follow. In the beginning it can be very helpful to have everyone meet face-to-face as this will help build trust and rapport among the team members.

Monitoring team members. Monitoring team members can be a big challenge, and the challenge is even greater if there is geographical distance between any or all members. Communication guidelines should be set up to allow managers to keep in touch and coach members throughout the project.

GUIDELINES FOR PROJECT SUCCESS

LEARNING AND DEVELOPMENT projects can be difficult to manage because of time pressure, ability to access resources, and the fact that different departments are often involved. Coordinating the project activities across departments and often across locations adds to the challenge. Having helped build a large-scale oil and gas complex, I can say with certainty that all these obstacles existed. While everyone is in the same time zone, some are working during the day while others are working the night shift. You have to deal with suppliers from all over the world who are in different time zones. I fondly remember going to back to my office just after midnight on a Thursday to have a discussion with a vendor in

Europe. And finally there's the challenge of having to coordinate the work and expertise of people from different disciplines.

The following are some guidelines for making projects successful:

- Make sure you have management support/sponsorship.
- Know the budget and the details of all expenses to ensure you will meet or come in under budget.
- Involve the end users of the project's outcome early and often; not only will this improve the outcome, but also it will increase the buy-in.
- Define in detail the project's outcome.
- Define in detail the tasks that need to be completed.
- Consider breaking the project up into phases (i.e., divide and conquer).
- Before you begin (i.e., before you say yes), ensure you will be able to have the number of team members you need, and that they have the requisite knowledge and skills or will be able to get the required training.

Ally, Cleveland-Innes, and Wiseman (2010) suggest breaking projects into six phases:

1. The project planning phase, where an overall plan is laid out, funding is secured, boundaries are identified, and stakeholders are identified and brought on board.
2. Analysis, the phase in which the learners' needs and levels are carefully determined so that the end product will be the best possible fit.
3. The design phase, which identifies the strategies and approaches that will be employed to achieve the desired final product.

4. The development phase, in which the product is created to the specifications of the design phase; this step involves the coming together and coordinating of the various disciplines required.

5. The implementation phase, where the new product is implemented parallel to a product it is replacing, or where the new product is implemented in a way in which the old product is completely removed and the new one is put in its place, or where the new product is phased in. Another option is to pilot in one location before replacing the old product in all locations. Or the product may be completely new, in which case some form of piloting would be wise. That way, if there are issues, not every potential user will be inconvenienced.

6. The support phase, which ensures there is help available for any potential problems, which could range from a learner's need of help to technical glitches.

THE REAL WORLD

WHILE I WAS working for a large oil and gas company, I put together a thorough project plan to introduce a new LMS, introduce a new delivery for safety training, and bring in a competency assurance process. I had management support for the project, so I was assured I would have the people and the resources needed. Just as we really got into this project, about six months into a two-year project, the price of oil crashed and all bets were off. Of course, everyone saw the value in what was being done, so management still wanted it done, only I did not get the people or resources that were in the original plan. In any project, no matter how well it is detailed and organized, and with all the support, events can happen in business that necessitate changes. In this case, there were major changes. The timeline was lengthened, and some items were eliminated. The learning from this is to always be prepared to make adjustments. As the saying goes, prepare for the worst and hope for the best.

CONCLUSION

THE FIRST STEP is to ensure you have management support. Be organized and detailed in every step of the planning and the process. Have a communication plan to ensure all team members stay in the loop. Resist scope creep at all costs. Finally, understand that in business the only constant is change, so be prepared to make adjustments to the project plan.

CHAPTER 17

Competency Assurance

INTRODUCTION

GOVERNMENT REGULATIONS ARE starting to insist that employers ensure their workers are competent to safely perform their jobs. In Canada, the criminal code was amended in 2004 with respect to workplace responsibilities. Part of its interpretation demands companies ensure that their workers can perform their work safely; this has boiled down to, "Can you prove that your workers are competent?" As a result, companies need to have a program in place where they can demonstrate that their employees are not just trained but also competent. For years, most companies have had good training programs as they have long since seen the value in having well-trained, skilled workers. However, now companies are moving beyond this to competency assurance programs where they measure if the training was learned and how well it is being applied as intended.

COMPETENCY

CHAPTER 6, ON needs analysis, defines competency as a combination of knowledge, skills, and attitude applied to perform a task. I've seen the term *attitude* replaced with various other terms, for example, *desire*. This is incorrect. I believe the reason people try to change the academic definition of competency is a result of the term *attitude* being perceived as negative. It is important to understand that in defining competency, the term *attitude* refers to the degree of assertiveness. Is a person who is applying the knowledge and skill doing so too timidly or too aggressively? For example, we could have a driver of a car who has knowledge about the rules of the road and the dynamics of how a car works and who has the utmost skill in operating the car in line with all his knowledge. However, when he arrives at a stop sign at a T-intersection, he is so timid that he won't make a left-hand turn until he can see no cars in either direction. We would have to rate such a person's competency for driving a car quite low. The same would apply for a highly knowledgeable and skilled driver with an attitude that's overly aggressive. To be highly competent, a driver needs to be conservatively assertive in her attitude. A football middle linebacker would need to be overly aggressive in his attitude to be highly competent. If we are considering knowledge, skills, and desire to define competency, we would need to rate a person who's too timid to be competent at driving as follows: If the driver had a strong desire to be a good driver and was as highly knowledgeable and skilled as the driver described above, then by the *desire* definition, we would conclude the driver is highly competent, yet clearly he would not be. Using the incorrect definition can lead you to deeming incompetent workers competent, and that could be deadly.

Technically, a competency relate to the smallest task that still requires both knowledge and skill to perform. In these terms, driving a car would be broken down into many smaller competencies, for example, coming to a stop, parallel parking, making a three-point turn, and controlling a skid. I do not believe it is necessary to break all the work tasks into their smallest components for the purposes of identifying what knowledge and which skills are required to perform the job. For example, driving car could be one competency with many elements. That said, if in doubt whether a competency is too big, break it down into smaller competencies. You cannot go wrong with competencies that are too small, but having competencies that are too big can pose problems.

Determine what tasks workers perform in a job, then determine from those tasks what competencies are required for the job. From the example in chapter 6 relating to the competency of installing piping comes the following list:

1a. Screwing pipe together.
1b. Run sections of piping.
1c. Install fitting plug.
1d. Correctly use piping tape and piping compound.
1e. Remove blind end from a hub.
1f. Install a two-inch flanged valve.
1g. Select correct spec pipe fittings for a given job.
1h. Select correct gaskets for a job.
1i. Select and use proper tools.
1j. Select and properly apply thread lubricants or lockers.

1k. Use rigging to support piping.

1l. Select and use the correct fasteners.

1m. Measure, cut, and thread a specified length of pipe.

1n. Install a union.

1o. Connect hose fittings to piping.

1p. Perform a hydro leak test.

If we examine 1a, screwing pipe together, we need to list out all the knowledge and skills required, and furthermore we need consider where the work will be performed and what knowledge and skills will be required to safely perform the tasks, for example:

Technical knowledge

- Number of turns to hand-tighten
- What rotational direction to use to tighten/loosen
- What type of thread compound is required
- What pipe specifications apply
- Proper tools used for tightening
- Proper use of tools
- Where to obtain and return the tools
- What constitutes thread damage

Technical skill

- Ability to adjust wrench size
- Ability to apply adequate force
- Coordination to connect fittings
- Hand–eye coordination to keep piping square

Safety knowledge

- What personal protective gear is required to prevent injury

- What body positioning is required
- Ability to recognize hazards (e.g., pinch points)
- What type of gloves should be worn, and what types should not

Safety skills

- Ability to don and doff personal protective gear
- Ability to maintain proper body positioning

This process would need to be repeated for each element. It will result in a lengthy but a bulletproof list from which to work.

Chapter 8 covered instructional design with a focus on teaching all the required knowledge and skills. For competency assurance, we use the same list, except it is used after instruction. The list is written in the form of criteria against which the trainee is assessed. The needs analysis (see chapter 6) identifies all the knowledge and skills a worker requires to perform the job effectively and safely. The needs analysis is used to create the instructional design. This ensures the workers are taught all the knowledge and skills required. The needs analysis is also used to create a complete list of the criteria a worker needs to be assessed against in order to prove his or her competence to effectively and safely perform the work.

The criteria for assessment need to be clearly defined. For example, to successfully park a car, the criteria might be as follows: (a) The driver must activate the turn signal in advance of slowing down to perform the parking maneuver. (b) The driver can only move the car back and forth two times before it is roughly centered in the parking space, and the car must be within ten inches of the curb. (c) The parking brake must be applied. Failure to meet these defined criteria will result in failure. If the criteria are not defined, the driver might go back and forth a dozen times and still be twenty inches from the curb, and still the driver would have to be passed.

If the driver were to fail, it would be unfair as she would not know to what level of proficiency she need to upgrade her ability.

In examining the list of knowledge and skills for installing piping, we might find that the knowledge and skill pertaining to the use of tools was identified in many other tasks within the needs analysis. As a result, a course on just the tools would be developed, and the use of the tools would only be referred to in the training on installing piping. Proving competency in the area of tools, and possibly some other elements, might be determined to be a prerequisite to be assessed for competence prior to assessing competency on the installing piping element.

At some point prior to drilling down into the knowledge and skills, a baseline or prerequisite set of knowledge and skills needs to be determined. For example, the worker needs to know that turning the piping clockwise will cause it to tighten. If we drill down, that means they'll need to know how to tell time on a nondigital watch or clock. Obviously, if we're dealing with adults, we expect them to already know this. Typically a determination would be made that the baseline of knowledge is high school level education, or a university or college degree or diploma would be used as a baseline of what knowledge and skills we can assume the workers to have.

VALIDATIONS

HAVING ALL THE criteria against which to assess a competency is half the battle. The second half is performing the competency assurance assessments or validations. Validating competencies raises a number of questions. Who can assess a worker's competency, and based on what do such people have this authority and ability? What process should they follow? How should the validations be documented? Beyond this, in many cases competencies will be items that cannot be very easily observed. I purposely chose the piping example because it is easy to describe and would be easy to observe and validate a worker on. This is not always the case, so how do we assure competency in those situations?

Ideally, a validator is someone who has been previously validated and is therefore recognized as having the knowledge, skills, attitude, and experience required. It is not always possible to have a validated person as a validator, for example, when the program is first started (i.e., the age-old chicken-and-egg scenario). I would suggest using a supervisor or someone from a leadership position who has expertise in the area. This person would be given training on the validator process and expectations, and he would perform the validations. This person does not need to be a subject matter expert, but he does need enough knowledge to know how tasks should be performed and what questions to ask to ensure the worker's competency.

If a task cannot be observed, then the validator needs to seek out evidence. Evidence is something that shows that something else exists or is true. It is a collection of things that are helpful in forming a conclusion or judgment. The higher the quality and/or the greater the quantity of evidence, the stronger the case that it exists or is true. Assurance is an indication that inspires confidence that the thing being validated is true. The evidence needs to make a strong or convincing case, showing that the person has the required level of knowledge and skill (competency) to be able to safely and successfully execute the task.

The most appropriate method of collecting evidence is always to concentrate on the most realistic work-based situation allowed by the work conditions. Ideally, a person's competency is validated by observing them performing the task. This not always possible for a variety of reasons, such as safety concerns, technical integrity of equipment, limited opportunity due to cyclical work, prohibitive cost, or inconvenience to a process or manufacturing facility. In these cases, the worker could perform a simulation of the task with the validator asking questions, or by having the worker provide a sketch and a description, or both. The knowledge aspect of competency can be assessed through written, verbal, or online tests. Typically a validation of a worker's competency involves a combination of these approaches.

For example, a millwright may have overhauled a centrifugal compressor last year. The evidence of competency would be the maintenance records indicating when the overhaul took place, how long it took, and who the millwright was who performed the overhaul. Operations records would serve as evidence showing that the compressor was started up and performed as expected and has now run for extended period of time without a failure, indicating the overhaul was performed correctly.

Another situation that often arises is when the worker could benefit from coaching. Does the validator help such a person pass the validation process by providing coaching, or does the validator wait until the validation is over to provide feedback, even if it means the worker will fail the validation? I think it is important for the worker to be able to demonstrate she is competent without any help, and this is also important for the business. If a large number of workers are failing their validations, then there is a problem that needs to be corrected. It could be that HR is hiring people who are not qualified, or perhaps improvements are needed in the training program, or one or more of a host of other possible causes. Helping people pass is not recommended for this reason, as it may hide other issues. That said, if a worker is being validated and he has performed a task technically correct but with coaching he could be even better, then by all means provide the coaching as it is at a very teachable moment.

For example, let's say you are teaching your sixteen-year old daughter how to drive. Once on the road, she approaches a stop sign and brakes very hard. The ABS comes close activating. Then once the traffic is clear and it is safe to proceed from the intersection, she does so, but by accelerating very hard, almost to the point of spinning the tires. Technically she did do everything right; she came to a controlled stop without locking up the tires, and she made sure the intersection was clear before proceeding. However, a better driver would slow down sooner and more gradually and then accelerate much more slowly, as this technique is both safer and a lot easier on the car. So, you would coach your daughter on this aspect. If she did not come to a full stop, you would need to point out that she failed. Then you would have her pull over, and you would ask her or tell her what she did wrong. And you wouldn't allow her to proceed until you were comfortable she understood the mistake and would not repeat it.

CONCLUSION

IT'S IMPORTANT TO have a thorough needs analysis. The instructional design must result in providing workers with the knowledge and skills they require to be successful and by extension for the company to be successful. The needs analysis provides a clearly defined list without any lacuna of skills and knowledge the workers require. Beyond the instructional design, creating a thorough competency assurance process is dependent upon the thoroughness of the needs analysis. As I've stated earlier in *The Handbook for Learning and Development Professionals*, there are no magic pills in learning and development; it is made up of rigorous, detailed, and highly organized work. Developing a quality needs analysis and competency assurance process requires a great deal of time and effort, and it can at times be monotonous, but it will produce the required results without fail.

CHAPTER 18

Learning Videos

INTRODUCTION

I CREATED MY first learning videos back in the early 1990s. Cameras and editing software have come a long way since then. It is much cheaper and easier to produce videos today. What I learned about creating learning videos has come from applying good learning principles to video, coupled with lots of learning by doing (learning from my many mistakes). I did have a good conversation about shooting learning videos a few years back at a learning conference in Toronto. I met a gentleman who worked for the BBC, and on a great many occasions he partnered up with a university (Oxford, if my memory serves me correctly) to shoot educational videos for the school. He told me of one time he was filming chimpanzees at a zoo as part of a documentary. The people working on this particular project were allowed to go right up to the bars that enclosed the chimpanzees so that the bars would not be in the photographs or video unless the producers wanted them to be. This gentleman said a female photographer he was working with was shooting pictures with her camera right through the bars. A young chimpanzee (a teenager) came right up to her looking curious and then suddenly snatched her camera bag. Then he scampered back into the enclosure and sat down on a rock. One of the zookeepers came up and told her not to worry. The zookeeper brought over a bottle of Coke. He explained this type of thing happens and that the chimpanzees will trade what they've taken for a bottle of Coke. The woman extended the bottle of Coke through the bars, and sure enough the teenage chimpanzee came over with the camera bag. Then suddenly he grabbed the Coke and, keeping the camera bag, scampered off back to the rock he was perched on. Immediately an older female chimpanzee who was curiously observing the scene got up, walked over to the teenaged chimpanzee, slapped him on the back of the head, took the camera bag over, and gave it to the photographer. We might be closer to chimpanzees than we care to believe.

There are steps to creating a quality video. The first is to write the script.

WRITING A SCRIPT

IF YOU SEARCH YouTube for how-to videos, you'll quickly see some very poorly made how-to videos. Most are real exercises in frustration when it comes to attempting to learn what you want to learn from them. While some of the videos are very good with good-quality images, steady zoom-ins where and when appropriate, and narration that is clear and precise, others are poor with shaky images, insufficient lighting, poor camera angles, and lots of dead time where the learner is left waiting and waiting for the next thing to happen. The key to creating good learning videos is to do the necessary work and planning ahead of time. Planning everything out and writing a good script is tedious and time-consuming, but when it comes time to narrate and shoot the video, the time spent in preparing properly will be well worth it. Plus, a good script helps greatly when you get to the video editing portion. There are many good products available for creating these types of videos, anything from Camtasia and Articulate Storyline to simple free downloadable video editing software. In the past video equipment was a big barrier to creating learning videos. Today most everyone has a smartphone, and most of today's smartphones shoot very good-quality video; you just need to make sure the phone is held steady. If you have access to professional equipment and personnel, all the better. The experience of a professional can be invaluable.

A few of years ago I was involved with a project for a professional hockey team (NHL). I worked with their nutritional experts. My role was to provide educational expertise in the development of several nutritional content videos for their players and prospective players playing in Europe and on various teams in North America. NHL teams all have their own video recording and editing personnel. The editing they were able to do made for very good learning videos and resulted in a lot less work for me. A person who uses video editing software regularly will be more efficient and capable than someone who only uses it once or twice per year. Beware that producing a video can be costly and time-consuming. In some cases an hour of video is shot, but only thirty seconds is used in the final product.

Here are the basic steps to follow for creating a learning (how-to) video:

1. Identify the specific learning topic, what exactly the video is going to be about. Be precise in defining this as it determines an exact starting point and a precise ending point. What content needs to be included, in what order does it need to be presented, and what can be excluded?
2. Identify the subject matter experts who will help you to develop the content.
3. Will you need a person or persons in the video to execute certain tasks? If so, you need to decide who they will be.
4. Determine what needs to be videoed for each step. Consider how much to zoom in or out. Do you need more than one video angle? What does the user need to see? Will you need to bring in extra lighting?
5. A good practice is to limit a static camera zoom and angle (a clip) to a maximum of four seconds long (aim for three), especially if there is no action taking place. If the narration for one particular item lasts ten seconds, show three different angles for three to three and a half seconds each. Next time you watch a sporting event on television, take note of how the camera angles and level of zoom constantly change.
6. Write a detailed script for each step/scene. The length of time that the narration takes typically determines how long the video scene(s) need(s) to be for each step.

LEARNING VIDEO SCRIPT EXAMPLE

THIS HOW-TO VIDEO is for showing how to change a car tire:

Scene 1
 Narration: Sometimes cars can get flat tires. (3 seconds)
 Video: Run 3 seconds of video clip VID_001 (video of a car with flat tire).

Scene 2
 Narration: The first step is locate the car's jack. (3 seconds)
 Video: Run 3 seconds of the video clip VID_002 (video from outside the car's trunk with woman pointing to the spare tire).

Scene 3
 Narration: The jack is typically stored in the trunk under the spare tire. (4 seconds)
 Run 2 seconds of video clip VID_003 (showing the wing nut that holds the spare tire in place being removed).
 Run 3 seconds of video clip VID_003b (showing the spare tire being lifted and placed to the side of the jack).

Scene 4
 Narration: Remove the jack and wheel nut wrench from the trunk. (3.5 seconds)
 Video: Run 3.5 seconds of the video clip VID_004 (woman removing the jack and wrench from the trunk).

Scene 5
 Narration: Place the jack under the car. (3.5 seconds)
 Run 4 seconds of the video clip VID_005 (jack being slid under the car; video angle is from the point of view of the person placing the jack under the car).

Scene 6

Narration: Make sure the jack's lifting pad will lift up against the lifting area provided under the car. (5 seconds)

Run 2 seconds of video VID_006 (video taken from ground level looking up at lifting area in the car's chassis with a finger pointing to and touching the lifting area).

Run 3 seconds of video VID_006b (video taken from ground level looking up at lifting area in the car's chassis with the jack's lifting pad being slid directly underneath it).

Scene 7

Narration: Use the wrench to turn the jack up, and watch that it comes up and lifts the car chassis lifting area. (6 seconds)

Run 3 seconds of video VID_007 followed by 3 seconds of VID_008 (showing the woman turning the wrench—one camera angle from just off to the side and behind the woman, and one angle from the side).

Scene 8

Narration: Use the jack to lift some of the weight off the wheel and tire. At this point you do not want to lift the tire completely off the ground. (7.5 seconds)

Run 3.5 seconds of VID_009 (showing the wrench being placed onto the jack and the wrench starting to be turned— close-up zoom).

Run 4 seconds of VID_009b (zooming out, showing woman turning the wrench and lifting the car up, then stopping and removing the wrench from the jack).

Scene 9

Narration: Next use the wrench to loosen each wheel nut one or two turns. By having some weight remain on the wheels and tires, the wheel will stay still while you are loosening the nuts. (9.6 seconds)

Run 3.2 seconds of each video VID_010, VID_011, and VID_012 (three different camera angles of the wheel nuts being loosened).

I won't carry on with the rest of the scenes as I think by now you get the idea of how to write a detailed script of the sort required for creating how-to learning videos.

CONCLUSION

THE KEY TO producing good-quality learning or how-to videos is in having a detailed script. The script comes from thoughtfully considering what the learning objectives are and how they would best be depicted in a video. Then create a detailed script that can be edited with the video clips and narration. If possible, have someone preview the video and discuss missing elements and/or improvements. Even videos with a good script are seldom perfect after the first edit.

APPENDICES

APPENDIX A

Bloom's Educational Objectives Taxonomy

1.00. **Knowledge**
1.10. Knowledge of specifics
1.11. Knowledge of terms
1.12. Knowledge of specific facts
1.20. Knowledge of ways and means of dealing with specifics
1.21. Knowledge of conventions
1.22. Knowledge of trends and sequences
1.23. Knowledge of classifications and categories
1.24. Knowledge of criteria
1.25. Knowledge of methodology
1.30. Knowledge of universals and abstractions in a field
1.31. Knowledge of principles and generalizations
1.32. Knowledge of theories and structure

2.00. **Comprehension** (grasping the meaning)
2.10. Translation (converting from one form to another)
2.20. Interpretation (explaining or summarizing material)

2.30. Extrapolation (extending the meaning beyond the data)

3.00. **Application** (using information in concrete situations)

4.00. **Analysis** (breaking down material into its parts)
4.10. Analysis of elements (identifying the parts)
4.20. Analysis of relationships (identifying the relationships)
4.30. Analysis of organizational principles (identifying the organization)

5.00. **Synthesis** (putting parts together into a whole)
5.10. Production of a unique communication
5.20. Production of a plan or proposed set of operations
5.30. Derivation of a set of abstract relations

6.00. **Evaluation** (judging the value of a thing for a given purpose using defined criteria)
6.10. Judgments in terms of internal evidence
6.20. Judgments in terms of external criteria

APPENDIX B

Krathwohl's Revised Educational Objectives Taxonomy

Knowledge Dimension
A. Factual knowledge—the basic elements that students must know to be acquainted with a discipline or to solve problems with it
    i. Knowledge of terminology
    ii. Knowledge of specific details and elements

B. Conceptual knowledge—the interrelationships among the basic elements within a larger structure that enables them to function together
    i. Knowledge of classifications and categories
    ii. Knowledge of principles and generalizations
    iii. Knowledge of theories, models, and structures

C. Procedural knowledge—how to do something; methods of inquiry and criteria for using skills, algorithms, techniques, and methods
  i. Knowledge of subject-specific skills and algorithms
  ii. Knowledge of subject-specific techniques and methods
  iii. Knowledge of criteria for determining when to use appropriate procedures

D. Metacognitive knowledge—knowledge of cognition in general, as well as awareness and knowledge of one's own cognition
  i. Strategic knowledge
  ii. Knowledge about cognitive tasks, including appropriate contextual and conditional knowledge
  iii. Self-knowledge

Cognitive Process Dimension

1.0. Remember—retrieve relevant knowledge from long-term memory
1.1. Recognize
1.2. Recall

2.0. Understand—determine the meaning of instructional messages, including oral, written, and graphic communications
2.1. Interpret
2.2. Exemplify
2.3. Classify
2.4. Summarize
2.5. Infer
2.6. Compare
2.7. Explain

3.0. Apply—carry out or use a procedure in a given situation
3.1. Execute
3.2. Implement

4.0. Analyze—break material into its constituent parts and detect how the parts relate to one another and to the overall structure or purpose
4.1. Differentiate
4.2. Organize
4.3. Attribute

5.0. Evaluate—make judgments based on criteria and standards
5.1. Check
5.2. Critique

6.0. Create—put elements together to form a novel coherent whole or to make an original product
6.1. Generate
6.2. Plan
6.3. Produce

APPENDIX C

Quellmalz's Framework Taxonomy

Recall. Remembering or recognizing key facts, definitions, concepts, etc.; repeating verbatim or paraphrasing information that has already been provided to the student.

Analysis. Understanding relationships between the whole and its component parts and between cause and effect; sorting and categorizing; understanding how things work and how the parts of something fit together; understanding causal relationships; getting information from charts, graphs, diagrams, and maps. Analysis is more than rote repetition; instead it involves reflectively structuring knowledge in new ways.

Comparison. Explaining how things are similar and how they are different. Comparisons may be either simple or complex. Simple comparisons are based on a small number of very obvious attributes. Complex comparisons require an examination of a more extensive set of attributes of two or more things. Comparisons start with the whole–part relationships in the analysis category and take them a step further.

Inference. Reasoning inductively or deductively. In deductive tasks, students reason from generalizations to specific instances and are asked to recognize or explain the evidence. In inductive tasks, students are given the evidence or details and are required to relate and integrate the information to come up with the generalization.

Evaluation. Expressing and defending an opinion. Evaluation tasks require students to judge quality, credibility, worth, or practicality using established criteria and then explain how the criteria are met or not met.

GLOSSARY OF TERMS

andragogy. A learning theory that relates to adult learning, specifically how adults learn vs. how children learn.

Cone of Experience. Developed by Dale Edgar (1946). A visual display depicting a taxonomy of (learning) experiences ranging from direct experience to pure abstraction.

curriculum design theory. Concerned with what should be learned.

design theory. Defined as being goal-oriented and normative. It attempts to identify the best methods for accomplishing goals.

distance education. Learners are separated by time and/or distance from the course content and the teachers.

instructional science. Focused on developing knowledge of both learning (descriptive theory) and instructional events (design theory).

learning objectives taxonomy. Classification of levels of knowledge.

m-learning. Mobile learning, that is, learning that takes place anywhere, anytime, by use of a handheld internet-connected technology, for example, smartphones (Apple iPhone, BlackBerry Torch, Motorola Android) and tablet PCs (iPad, PlayBook).

motivation. A force, stimulus, or influence that acts on a person to generate an emotional reaction to move toward something.

needs analysis. A formal process for determining what a student needs to learn to meet predescribed learning objectives (job requirements).

relevance. The more meaningful something is to a person's goals, the greater the relevance it has.

self-efficacy. The amount of confidence or level of belief a person has in feeling he or she can accomplish something.

REFERENCES

Ally, M., M. Cleveland-Innes, and C. Wiseman. 2010. "Managing Distance Education Projects in a Telework Environment." *Journal of Distance Education* 24, no. 1: 1–20.

Artino, A. R. Jr. 2010. "Online or Face-to-Face Learning? Exploring Personal Factors that Predict Students' Choice of Instructional Format." *Internet and Higher Education* 13, no. 4: 272–76.

Artino, A. R. Jr., and J. M. Stephens. 2006. "Learning Online? Motivated to Self Regulate?" *Academic Exchange Quarterly* 10, no. 4: 176–82.

Bandura, A. 1982. "Self-Efficacy Mechanism in Human Agency." *American Psychologist* 37, no. 2: 122–47.

———. 1997. *Self-Efficacy: The Exercise of Control.* New York: Freeman.

Baudrillard, J. 1983. *Simulations.* New York: Semiotext(e).

Bloland, H. G. 1995. "Postmodernism and Higher Education." *The Journal of Higher Education* 66, no. 5: 521–59.

Bloom, B. S., M. D. Engelhart, E. J. Furst, W. H. Hill, and D. R. Krathwohl. 1956. *Taxonomy of Educational Objectives: Handbook I—Cognitive Domain.* New York: David McKay.

Bolden, R. 2011. *Distributed Leadership.* Accessed August 26, 2019. http://www.bookrags.com/tandf/distributed-leadership-tf/.

Brehm, B. A. 2004. *Health and Fitness Handouts for Your Clients.* Champaign, IL: Human Kinetics.

Bruer, J. T. 1998. "Let's Put Brain Science on the Back Burner." *National Association of Secondary School Principals Bulletin* (May 1998): 9–19.

Bryson, B. 2004. *A Short History of Nearly Everything.* Toronto: Anchor.

Caffarella, R. S. 1994. *Program Planning for Adult Learners.* San Francisco: Jossey-Bass.

Cho, K. W., J. Altarriba, and M. Popiel. 2014. "Mental Juggling: When Does Multitasking Impair Reading Comprehension?" *Journal of General Psychology* 142, no. 2: 90–105.

Cornett, C. E. 1986. *Learning through Laughter.* Bloomington, MN: Phi Delta Kappa Educational Foundation.

Crowder, K. D. 2015. "Examining the Outcomes of Mobile Learning Used to Train Elite-Level Hockey Players as Measured by Kirkpatrick's Evaluation Model." EdD diss., Athabasca University.

Caulfield, T. 2012. *A Cure for Everything.* Toronto: Penguin Group.

Derrida, J. 1976. *Of Grammatology.* Baltimore: Johns Hopkins University Press.

DeTure, M. 2004. "Cognitive Style and Self-Efficacy: Predicting Student Success in Online Distance Education." *American Journal of Distance Education* 18, no. 1: 21–38.

Driscoll, M. P. 2000. *Psychology of Learning for Instruction.* Boston: Allyn & Bacon.

Duff, A., and T. Duffy. 2002. "Psychometric Properties of Honey & Mumford's Learning Styles Questionnaire (LSQ)." *Personality and Individual Differences* 33, no. 1: 147–63.

Duke University. 2013. "Bioelectricity: A Quantitative

Approach." *First MOOC summary*. Accessed August 26, 2019. http://dukespace.lib.duke.edu/dspace/bitstream/handle/10161/6216/Duke_Bioelectricity_MOOC_Fall2012.pdf.

Edgar, D. 1946. *Audio-Visual Methods in Teaching*. New York: Dryden Press.

Fahy, P. J., and M. Ally. 2005. "Student Learning Style and Asynchronous Computer-Mediated Conferencing (CMC) Interaction." *American Journal of Distance Education* 19, no. 1: 5–22.

Fleming, N. D., and C. Mills. 1992. "Not Another Inventory, Rather a Catalyst for a Reflection." *To Improve the Academy* 11: 137–55.

Ford, M. E. 1992. *Motivating Humans: Goals, Emotions, and Personal Agency Beliefs*. Newbury Park, CA: Sage.

Foucault, M. 1979. *Discipline and Punish*. New York: Vintage Books.

Gardner, H. 1983. *Frames of Mind: The Theory of Multiple Intelligences*. New York: Basic Books.

Garner, I. 2000. "Problems and Inconsistencies with Kolb's Learning Styles." *Educational Psychology* 20, no. 3: 341–48.

Gladwell, M. 2008. *Outliers*. New York: Back Bay Books / Little, Brown and Company.

Grasha, A. F., and S. W. Riechmann. 1974. "A Rationale to Developing and Assessing the Construct Validity of a Student Learning Styles Scale Instrument." *Journal of Psychology* 87: 213–23.

Green, L. W., and M. W. Kreuter. *Health Promotion Planning: An Educational and Environmental Approach*. 2nd ed. Mountain View, MO: Mayfield, 1991.

Gronlund, N. E. *Assessment of Student Achievement*. 6th ed. Needham Heights, MA: Allyn & Bacon, 1998.

Haihong, H., and J. Gramling. 2009. "Learning Strategies for

Success in a Web-Based Course." *Quarterly Review of Distance Education* 10, no. 2: 123–34.

Hannafin, M., H. Hannafin, and B. Gabbitas. 2009. "Re-Examining Cognition during Student-Centered Web-Based Learning." *Educational Technology Research and Development* 57: 767–85.

Harris, A. 2008. "Distributed Leadership: According to the Evidence." *Journal of Educational Administration* 46, no. 2: 172–88.

Hazy, J. K. 2008. "Toward a Theory of Leadership in Complex Systems: Computational Modeling Exploration." *Nonlinear Dynamics, Psychology, and Life Sciences* 12, no. 3: 281–310.

Honey, P., and A. Mumford. 1982. *Manual of Learning Styles.* London: P Honey.

Kane, R. 1985. *Free Will and Values.* Albany, NY: State University of New York Press.

Kanuka, H., and N. Nocente. 2003. "Exploring the Effects of Personality Type on Perceived Satisfaction with Web-Based Learning in Continuing Professional Development." *Distance Education* 24, no. 2: 227–45.

Keller, J. M. 1987. "Development and Use of the ARCS Model of Motivational Design." *Journal of Instructional Development* 10, no. 3: 2–10.

Kirkpatrick, D. L. *Evaluating Training Programs.* 2nd ed. San Francisco: Berrett-Koehler, 1998.

———. 1959a. "Techniques for Evaluating Training Programs: Reaction." *American Society for Training and Development Journal* 13: 3–9.

———. 1959b. "Techniques for Evaluating Training Programs: Learning." *American Society for Training and Development Journal* 13: 21–26.

———. 1960a. "Techniques for Evaluating Training Programs:

Behavior." *American Society for Training and Development Journal* 14: 13–18.

———. 1960b. "Techniques for Evaluating Training Programs: Learning." *American Society for Training and Development Journal* 14: 28–32.

———. *Evaluating Training Programs: The Four Levels.* 2nd ed. San Francisco: Berrett-Koehler, 1998.

Knowles, M. S. 1970. *The Modern Practice of Adult Education: Andragogy versus Pedagogy.* Englewood Cliffs, NJ: Prentice.

———. 1989. *The Making of an Adult Educator.* San Francisco: Jossey-Bass.

Knowles, M. S., E. F. Holton, and R. A. Swanson. *The Adult Learner.* 8th ed. New York: Routledge, 2015.

Kolb, D. 1984. *Experience as the Source of Learning and Development.* Englewood Cliffs, NJ: Prentice Hall.

Krathwohl, D. R. 2002. "A Revision of Bloom's Taxonomy: An Overview." *Theory into Practice* 41, no. 4: 212–18.

Lan, W. Y. 1996. "The Effects of Self-Monitoring on Students' Course Performance, Use of Learning Strategies, Attitude, Self-Judgment Ability, and Knowledge Representation." *Journal of Asynchronous Learning Networks* 4, no. 1: 23–32.

Latchem, C., and D. E. Hanna. 2001. *Leadership for 21st Century Learning.* New York: Routledge.

Leacock, S. 1937. *Humour and Humanity: An Introduction to the Study of Humour.* London: Thornton Butterworth.

Lin, C. H., and S. Gregor. 2006. "Designing Websites for Learning and Enjoyment: A Study of Museum Experiences." *International Review of Research in Open and Distance Learning* 7, no. 3. http://www.irrodl.org/index.php/irrodl/article/view/364.

Lynch, R. 2003. "The Relationship between Academic Self-Regulation and Online Distance Education." PhD diss.,

University of Southern California. ProQuest (UMI no. 3116750).

Lyotard, J. F. 1984. *The Postmodern Condition*. Minneapolis: University of Minnesota Press.

Management Study Guide.com. 2011. "Transformational Leadership Theory." Accessed August 26, 2019. http://www.managementstudyguide.com/transformational-leadership.htm.

Maslow, A. H. *Motivation and Personality*. 3rd ed. New York: Harper & Row, 1987.

McAuley, E., and B. Blissmer. 2000. "Self-Efficacy Determinants and Consequences of Physical Activity." *Exercise and Sport Sciences Reviews* 28, no. 2: 85–88.

Mickelson, J. J., W. E. Kaplan, and A. E. MacNeily. 2009. "Active Learning: A Resident's Reflection on the Impact of a Student-Centred Curriculum." *Canadian Urological Association Journal* 3, no. 5: 399–402.

Moan, E. R., and M. I. Dereshiwsky. 2002. "Identifying Factors that Predict Student Engagement in Web-Based Course Work." *USDLA Journal* 16, no. 1. Accessed December 1, 2017. https://www.learntechlib.org/p/93567/.

Moore, M. G. *Handbook of Distance Learning*. 3rd ed. New York: Routledge, 2013.

Pasquale, J. 2009. "Impact Study of a Central Lines Simulation Training Using Kirkpatrick's Four-Level Evaluation Model." PhD. diss., Pennsylvania. ProQuest (UMI no. 3374183).

Peterson, J. 2018. *12 Rules for Life*. Toronto: Random House.

Price, L. 2004. "Individual Differences in Learning: Cognitive Control, Cognitive Styles, and Learning Style." *Educational Psychology* 24, no. 5: 683–98.

Quellmalz, E. S. 1987. *Developing Reasoning Skills*. New York: Freeman.

Reigeluth, C. M., and A. A. Carr-Chellman. 2009. *Instructional-Design Theories and Models*, vol. 3. New York: Routledge, Taylor, and Francis.

Santo, S. A. 2001. *Virtual Learning, Personality, and Learning Styles.* PhD. diss., University of Virginia.

Schellens, T., and M. Valcke. 2000. "Re-Engineering Conventional University Education: Implications for Students' Learning Styles." *Distance Education* 21, no. 2: 261–384.

Schilcht, J., J. Godin, and D. C. Camaione. 1999. "How to Help Your Clients Stick with an Exercise Program: Build Self-Efficacy to Promote Exercise Adherence." *ACSM Health and Fitness Journal* 3, no. 6: 27–31.

Schlegel, C., U. Woermann, M. Shaha, J. Rethans, and C. van der Vleuten. 2011. "Effects of Communication Training on Real Practice Performance: A Role-Play Module versus a Standard Patient Module." *Journal of Nursing Education* 51, no. 1: 16–22.

Schunk, D. H., and P. A. Ertmer. 1999. "Self-Regulatory Process during Computer Skill Acquisition: Goal and Self-Evaluative Influences." *Journal of Educational Psychology* 91, no. 2: 251–60.

Schunk, D. H., and C. W. Swartz. 1993. "Goals and Process Feedback: Effects on Self-Efficacy and Writing Achievement." *Contemporary Educational Psychology* 18, no. 3: 337–54.

Scott, C. 2010. "The Enduring Appeal of 'Learning Styles.'" *Australian Journal of Education* 54, no. 1: 5–17.

Shih, E. S., and D. Mills. 2007. "Setting the New Standard with Mobile Computing in Online Learning." *International Review of Research in Open and Distance Learning* 8, no. 2. Accessed August 26, 2019. http://www.irrodl.org/index.php/irrodl/article/view/361/929.

Siemens, G. 2004 "Connectivism: A Learning Theory for the Digital Age." Accessed August 26, 2019. http://www.elearnspace.org/Articles/connectivism.htm.

Skinner, B. F. 1953. *Science and Human Behavior*. New York: Free Press.

Solms, M., and O. Turnbull. 2002. *The Brain and the Inner World: An Introduction to the Neuroscience of the Subjective Experience*. New York: Other Press.

Stogdill, R. M. 1974. *Handbook of Leadership: A Survey of the Literature*. New York: Free Press.

Stokking, K. M. 1996. "Levels of Evaluation: Kirkpatrick, Kaufman and Keller, and Beyond." *Human Resource Development Quarterly* 7, no. 2: 179–83.

Sumner, M., D. Bock, and G. Giamartino. 2006. "Exploring the Linkage between the Characteristics of IT Project Leaders and Project Success." *Information Systems Management* 23, no. 4: 43–50.

Terrell S. R. 2002. "The Effect of Learning Style on Doctoral Course Completion in a Web-Based Learning Environment." *The Internet and Higher Education* 5: 345–52.

———. 2003. "Supporting Different Learning Styles in an Online Learning Environment: Does It Really Matter in the Long Run?" *Distance Education* 24, no. 2: 141–58.

Tough, A. 1971. *The Adult's Learning Projects: A Fresh Approach to Theory and Practice in Adult Learning*. Toronto: OISE.

Tuckman, B. W. 1965. "Developmental Sequence in Small Groups." *Psychological Bulletin* 63, no. 6: 384–99.

Value Based Management.net. 2016. "Contingency Leadership Theory." Accessed August 26, 2019. http://www.valuebasedmanagement.net/methods_contingency_theory.html.

Vygotsky, L. S. 1978. *Mind in Society: Development of Higher Psychological Processes*. Edited by M. Cole, V. John-Steiner, S. Scribner, and E. Souberman. Cambridge, MA: Harvard University Press.

Wang, A. Y., and M. H. Newlin. 2002. "Predictors of Web-Student Performance: The Role of Self-Efficacy and Reasons for Taking an On-Line Class." *Computers in Human Behavior* 18, no. 2: 151–63.

Wosnitza, M., and S. Volet. 2005. "Origin, Direction, and Impact of Emotions in Social Online Learning." *Learning and Instruction* 15, no. 5: 449–64.

Zimmerman, B. J. 1990. "Self-Regulated Learning and Academic Achievement: An Overview." *Educational Psychologist* 25, no. 1: 3–17.

Zimmerman, B. J., and A. Kitsantas. 1999. "Acquiring Writing Revision Skill: Shifting from Process to Outcome Self-Regulatory Goals." *Journal of Educational Psychology* 91, no. 2: 241–50.

Zimmerman, B. J., and M. Martinez-Pons. 1986. "Development of a Structured Interview for Assessing Student Use of Self-Regulated Learning Strategies." *American Educational Research Journal* 23, no. 4: 614–28.

Printed in the United States
By Bookmasters